WINNING IN
SPORTS BUSINESS

David,

Thanks so much for being
a part of this book! I believe there's
a lot of value in it & you're a huge
part of that!

-Michael Rosile

WINNING IN SPORTS BUSINESS

MICHAEL RASILE

NEW DEGREE PRESS

WINNING IN SPORTS BUSINESS

ISBN   978-1-63676-608-9 *Paperback*
        978-1-63676-272-2 *Kindle Ebook*
        978-1-63676-273-9 *Ebook*

Table of Contents

Introduction

How long did it take for you to get your dream job? If you haven't gotten it yet, what are you willing to do to get it? Between the difficult journey and bumps along the road, every "overnight success" takes about fifteen years.

Mark Simon is well-known for his role on *Baseball Tonight* at ESPN, but it's not like he showed up one day and said, "I'm Mark Simon, I deserve this job." He worked very hard to get to where he is today. We'll dive deeper into his story later on during this book, but I think he is the perfect starting example to show the dedication he put into his career path and where it helped him end up.

Mark earned the opportunity to spend over fifteen years at ESPN, the worldwide leader in sports, by giving value to others, being nice to those around him, and working hard at a low cost to get into the business. Mark graduated from The College of New Jersey; and while he was there, he took up a part time job at a local paper to juice up his portfolio. He worked hard, but never received that full-time job at the newspaper, so he started to think about his dream job. Mark was an avid reader of ESPN. com and of the columnist Jayson Stark—who publishes an article each week with some interesting baseball stats and facts. A short period of time before this, he wrote a note to the legendary baseball writer about Charlie Brown and a lead he let up in a comic strip, referencing an MLB game that happened earlier in the week. By adding value to Jayson by giving him a funny statistic that his readers would enjoy, Mark realized he could now ask Jayson for help when looking for a job at ESPN. He wrote him once, why not try to go 2-2? So, Mark wrote Jayson once more asking for the name of the hiring manager at ESPN for *Baseball Tonight*.

It doesn't sound like much, but many people fail to do what Mark accomplished. Mark added value through a funny anecdote that he thought Jayson's readers would enjoy, which is something few think to do. He broke into ESPN, and from there, he let his hard work do the rest of the talking. Mark spent over fifteen amazing years at ESPN before eventually moving on to Sports Info Solutions, where he gets to work directly with your favorite broadcasters and media personalities.

Early on, so many people told me I had to be cutthroat to make it in the world of sports and business—but Mark shows a different path. I wondered if he was unique or part of a much larger trend, and what I learned has changed the entire way I see the sports and entertainment world.

"Sports Industry" is a term that most people understand when they hear it, but can't quite put their finger on a definition. I'm not here to define the industry because there are many different facets, and there is a subjective nature to it. When I speak about the sports industry throughout this book, I will be referring to the broadest possible sense of the term to encompass just about every aspect of the industry. This includes but isn't limited to: teams, leagues, athletes, sponsors and partners, agencies, marketing companies, venues, events, and even hot dog sales. With this view, the estimated market size of the entire sports industry in 2018 was over one trillion dollars—twelve zeros—about 1.3 trillion dollars to be a bit more precise, worldwide. The estimated size of the sports themselves is over five hundred billion dollars. Soccer is far and away the biggest of all the sports, with an estimated market share of about forty-three percent and American football in a distant second with around thirteen percent of the financial sports market. There are also eight thousand indigenous sports and sporting games that collectively barely make up eight percent of the market, many of these sports we have never heard of, and probably never will. [1] With so much money, coverage, and eyeballs, it's not surprising so many people want to be part of the industry.

After the "major leagues" of sports, we can also point to the youth aspect of sports—where we all learned how to play—as another huge factor in this equation. In the United States alone, over sixty million kids play youth sports in some capacity, helping create a multi-billion-dollar industry itself. And it is expected to continue to grow, with the estimated size of the industry expected to make it to eighty million by 2030. [2]

A few key drivers for the sports market are media companies like ESPN, sponsorships and brands like Nike, the leagues themselves, sports betting properties, and booming areas like esports. Throughout this book, you

1   "How big is the sports industry?," SportyCo, accessed September 9, 2020.
2   "How Large Is the Industry?," i9 Sports, accessed September 9, 2020.

will hear stories and experiences from people within each of these areas! Before the advent of social media, and the Internet before that, the sports industry may have looked like a gated community where only few were allowed in. Now, with much more transparency in this media market and many other changes, the opportunities have continued to open up. With a potential one trillion dollars up for grabs, more and more people are finding their way into the industry in new and interesting ways. [3]

A common theme for many outside observers of the sports industry is how cutthroat and backstabbing the people in the industry can be. Most of this belief, I think, comes from sports and entertainment lawyers and agents. What is portrayed in television and movies can be the case in some situations, but this doesn't mean it's the truth. Obviously, some of it has to be true, but movies like *Jerry Maguire* are not the best way to assume how a job is done. Doing whatever it takes, walking over others, and making illegal deals happens in all industries, but for some reason it's the expected norm in the sports world. Agents are looked at as people who will do whatever they can to make the money they want.

Screaming at others, berating their employees, and spreading lies about their competition might seem commonplace, but I've found that isn't quite the case. The best way to make it in the sports industry is by being a good person, helping others, and working hard.

I'm compelled to write this book because over the last few months, I've gotten some amazing opportunities. I have a

---

3   "Sports Industry Statistic and Market Size Overview, Business and Industry Statistics," Plunkett Research, accessed September 9, 2020.

podcast called *For the Love of Sports*, where I speak with people all over the sports industry to understand how they broke in, why they love what they do, and how they take it to the top on a daily basis. Through interviews, I've had the pleasure of speaking with high-ranking executives, athletes, and entrepreneurs who are all within the sports industry. By asking questions, being curious, and being more interested than interesting, opportunities started coming my way. I'm a big believer in networking and creating relationships with like-minded people within any industry. You never know how you'll be able to help somebody else, and helping others is one of my favorite things to do.

For me, this means helping others without expecting anything in return. Do it because it's the right thing to do, not because you're looking for them to give you something back or because they can help you. When you're out networking with all different types of people, you need to be listening to what they say because, at some point in the conversation, they'll let you know how you can help. And that's how you can be of value to others, just listen.

I am qualified to write this book because of my experiences and the process of learning from many of the experts you will hear from. I personally run a company where I help athletes with sponsorships and endorsements. Through this, I have spoken with people all over the world about the ever-growing sports industry to gain more knowledge and situational awareness within the space.

As I said before, opportunities started to come my way when I continued to ask questions and learn about the experts I've spoken with. One of the coolest opportunities for me was when I interviewed Jason Mezrahi of *Win Daily Sports*. During the interview, he let me know that the co-host of his *SiriusXM Radio Show* recently had a baby and was not able to be on the show anymore. He liked my style of conversation and knowledge of fantasy sports and, after talking occasionally over a few weeks, he asked me to join him on the internationally broadcasted show. I was able to provide value to Jason by sharing the story of his business on my show and just happened to conduct his interview at the perfect time.

My path has been similar to Mark's in that I was able to add value to Jason by sharing his story with the world and highlighting his business. I then added value again in a more direct fashion by helping him in a time of need with his radio show. Finding people in any industry that are higher up the totem pole than you to help with no expectation for anything in return has helped me and many others in the industry get closer to where we want to be. If you can be of service to them, they may just ask for your help like how Jason asked me, or you can make the initiative like Mark did when he sent the story to Jayson Stark. But you have to understand that you will need to contribute no matter what.

The problem with people thinking that you have to be cutthroat to make it in the sports industry is that it's not the only way. Yes, some people will act and behave poorly and make it to the top, but skeletons fall out of the closet, and people will always remember how you made them feel. I believe that being of value to others, doing the right thing, putting in some free or low-cost work, and working hard are the best ways to make it in the sports industry. Free and low-cost work, especially when you're young, is the best way to learn. Not all situations are created equal, as you'll see later on, but if there is someone you trust and believe in, then working under him or her can be much more valuable than the money you think you "should" be earning.

This book will provide you some behind the scenes stories from some of the smartest people in the industry. From mega agents like David Meltzer, the former CEO of the most notable sports agency in the world, to Mark Taffet, the person who started HBO Sports Pay-Per-View, this book is jam-packed with great stories, great people, and great information.

If you're a high school or college student looking for a way into the sports industry and you're not sure how to do it, this book can help. If you're a career changer looking to finally do something you love with your life, this book can help! Or if you're just someone who loves sports and the stories behind them, you'll find enjoyment in this book. With the notable names and stories, learning how the sausage is made can be the most enjoyable part. You'll learn how many of these industry professionals and experts broke in, and what they did to take it to the top. First, we're going to need to learn more about competition, sports, and sports business to see exactly how we can make the biggest impact for ourselves and the other people within the industry.

PART 1

CHAPTER 1

Competitive Nature of the Sports Industry

———

Competition and sports go hand in hand. Two athletes, two teams, multiple players competing to win (unless it's soccer, then they're competing to tie) and see who can come out on top. It shouldn't be a surprise that a massive competition exists on the business side of the sports industry as well.

Whether it's an entry-level ticket sales position, gameday operations intern, or at the highest levels of partnership sales, the competition is there, and it is palpable. This competitiveness even comes to fruition with the broadcast crew that televises the game for us, as you'll hear later.

In this book, I wanted to explore and determine if the ruthless nature of certain jobs is the best way to make it to the top, or if being nice is the way to go. How much does the competition of the sport bleed over into the business aspect? How does this competitive nature affect the product that we see on the field? What can you learn from this and rise to the top?

But first, I want to ask the question "Does it pay to be a 'bad guy' in the sports industry?" Let's define what a "bad guy" is so we're all on the same page. To me, a "bad guy" is someone who doesn't take other people into account, who will do terrible things to get the job done; someone who will crawl over others and shove them back down before sticking out his or her hand to help someone else up. With that being said, does it pay to be a "bad guy" in the sports industry?

To understand the answer, we have to take a look at why we're even asking that question. We probably don't ask this about other industries where people seem civilized. Does it pay to be a "bad guy" in consumer packaged goods? Does it pay to be a "bad guy" in video production? Does it pay to be a "bad guy" in banking? Well, scratch that last one because the answer is still up in the air... But with many of those other industries, you would not normally assume the people are bad.

Most people assume that those working in the sports industry got there through backstabbing others. I think a big reason for that is how shady the sports betting industry may have been back in the day (we'll find it's not like that anymore) and how some of these careers were portrayed in movies. Sports betting has always been looked at as the underbelly of the sports industry, with mob bosses paying off players to throw a game and their cronies going around causing mayhem if something doesn't work in their favor. It also doesn't help that the

United States has only recently allowed states to have legalized sports betting. Just because something is illegal, doesn't mean it's bad. The rest of the world has had legal sports betting for years with very few major scandals (except Soccer).

Sports agents are looked at by many as the scum of the earth. Their slicked back hair, overpriced suits, nasty attitudes, and fake tans never really did much to lead people to believe that they are good people, or "nice guys." Of course, not all sports agents are like this but there are a few who are. Some may look like this to "look the part," but only because society dictates it.

Aside from this aspect of sports agents, a little movie came along during the '90s called *Jerry Maguire* where Tom Cruise played the titular character who has an idea to help fewer clients, be more honest with them, and help them in more ways. So, what happens when he has this idea? He is promptly let go from the agency he's working with. Sounds like a good idea when you lay it out, but the sports agent world is not about being any of those things, it's only about *money*. Now, we know it's a movie and Tom Cruise does win in the end (he probably also has a scene where he runs a lot, does his own stunts, and saves the day), but this still helped lay the groundwork for the industry to be looked at as cutthroat. Considering Jerry Maguire was a "rogue" character, the assumption would be that he is unlike the rest of the industry, he is the exception to the rule.

This movie was also such a hit that insane amounts of people started to become NFL-certified sports agents.

The played-up glamour and celebrity of the movie painted an awesome picture where normal "nice guys" could get their licenses and certifications and start helping superstar athletes. "Over the next five years, the full impact of what the movie inspired became clear. Five years before the movie, there were roughly four hundred registered NFL agents. Five years after? More than one thousand, and that was even as the NFL Players Association more than doubled the fee to certify an agent."[4]

With so many new people to the industry and the assumption of "nice guys finish last," many bad guys did come out of this. But many nice guys did too. Jerry Maguire is based off real life super-agent Leigh Steinberg, who ended up running Leigh Steinberg Entertainment, one of America's most notable sports agencies. Lucky for us, I have the second CEO of Leigh Steinberg Entertainment in this book for us to learn from.

Aside from pop culture and movies that play up the good, and bad, parts of the lifestyle, there is much more to be examined. Three aspects I would like to look into are: sports themselves are competitive, many people who work in the sports industry played sports in some capacity, and the sports industry is male-dominated.

I am a true believer in competition; it breeds excellence. To define further, competition is often described as a contest, or a process of contesting, between two or more parties for a scarce resource or good. The supply of jobs and resources in sports, particularly in areas like

---

4   Daren Rovell, "How 'Jerry Maguire' ruined the sports agency industry," ESPN, Dec 13, 2016.

representation, is thin. Consider an agency where there is a limited number of high-end athletes and a limited number of brands, events, and teams that are willing to pay top dollar for them. Without those top-tier athletes and brand connections, your job becomes much harder. At this point, a "shortcut" seems like a great option to just get ahead of the game. Lying, cheating, stealing, and spreading rumors all can be used to aid your mission of climbing to the top, but rarely does it work out when you use these tactics.

Consider sports with rules and regulations governed by referees on the playing field; the sports business industry doesn't have someone at all meetings paying attention to how each player is conducting themselves. Some people will do what they're not supposed to and try to get away with it, others will tattle, and some will simply follow the rules. Since the sports business industry doesn't have these rules and referees, it makes it a bit harder to navigate at times and understand what's the best course of action.

Just like in sports, the sports business industry does have a grand goal to work toward. For teams, it's a trophy of some kind; for sports business professionals, it's a job or title they would like to achieve. Being competitive outside of sports does not translate in quite the same way as it does within sports, though, many times leading to negative outcomes. Competition does breed excellence and fighting against yourself isn't going to get you as far as competing with the other businesspeople around you. "Norman Triplett found that cyclists performed faster when they were racing against other cyclists than when they were racing against the clock." Unfortunately, many of the studies since have shown that high levels of competition actually bring out negative effects in those competing when not based in sports. "Subsequent research has demonstrated that for most types of tasks in most situations, competition leads to poorer performance. The exceptions are simple tasks or rudimentary skills, the performance of which can be facilitated through competition."[5]

I personally believe some level of competition is necessary within all aspects of life, but it does lead to question if the highly competitive nature of sports bleeding into business brings out negatives in those working within it. It is often drilled into an athlete's head that he or she needs to do whatever it takes to win, and the higher the level, the higher competition which leads to more glory, fame, and the potential for money. This level of competition can absolutely lead to some unwarranted ways of going about your sports business career.

Heightened levels of competition are driven by the fact that so many athletes end up working in sports, and many of them are male.

There are about 7.3 million athletes within the high school level of sports, and about six percent of them move on to the NCAA system at all three division levels. Of that six percent, or about four hundred ninety-two thousand, famously less than two percent of those athletes play their sport professionally. This leaves a significant

5   "Competition in Sports," Psychology Research and Reference, accessed September 9, 2020.

amount of people who have played sports until they were about eighteen years old and now do not have the same competitive outlet they had before. Well over the seven million people who do not make it to professional sports might still have the desire to be part of the sports world, leading many of these athletes into coaching, ticket sales, operations, and marketing, among other opportunities within the sports industry. [6]

Many of these athletes will be fueling their competitive nature in some way, shape, or form within the sports industry through business. Again, this is not a bad thing; I'm on the side of competition. Some athletes will train, learn, and execute like they did on the field, but there will also be some who take the shortcut to achieve their goals.

Since there is a high percentage of male athletes in the sports industry, there is also a higher level of competition. An interesting aspect of competition actually comes after the competition is over and whether or not someone decides to compete again. Through multiple studies, it is found that after losing a competition, a man's testosterone level can increase or decrease. "seventy percent of those whose testosterone levels increased chose to compete again, but eighty percent of those whose levels decreased declined to compete again."[7]

"When testosterone levels increase, we seem to become more dominant and driven to gain status. But when testosterone levels drop, we seem to become more

6   "Estimated probability of competing in college athletics," NCAA, accessed September 9,2020.

7   Medical Press "Men's testosterone levels predict competitiveness," University of Texas at Austin, accessed: September 9, 2020.

submissive."[8] This behavior goes hand in hand with the stereotypical "male machismo" often depicted in movies and pop culture—more so the angry-sore-loser aspect, but all these stereotypes are encompassing. These studies show that whether a male's testosterone goes up or down is almost predetermined, dependent on the stress levels before the competition even started. Higher stress levels lead to a decrease in testosterone, and lower stress levels lead to an increase of testosterone.

"The researchers were surprised to find changes in testosterone levels did not predict who would want to compete again among the men who won the competition. The researchers speculate winners may not be interested in facing the same opponent because the rematch might result in a loss."[9] Unlike in sports where the probability to play a team multiple times a season or a year is very common, in the business world, you are rarely going up against the same opponent; again, the movies lie to us. Yes, I'm sure it does come down to two of the best in their respective profession competing for the top athletes, biggest deals, or must lucrative opportunities, but there are too many other factors involved to place the "blame" on one thing. More likely, an agent would feel the athlete is the competition, trying to sign him or her to a deal and competing against the other agent who is trying to do the same.

It may sound weird that males with less stress will be the ones that are more competitive due to higher levels of testosterone because we are talking about highly

8   Ibid.
9   Ibid.

stressful positions. But as we know, competition isn't everything. Sports business professionals can do many other things that aren't looked at as competition and can lead to longer, more enjoyable careers.

In a male-dominated industry where many of the people working in it come from a competitive background, it's not too hard to see how the competitive nature of the sports industry is shaped. With pop culture making the "backstabbing" nature even more prevalent and seemingly commonplace, it's not too hard to see why so many people may choose to go the "bad guy" route after entering or being in the industry for a while. Of course, certain career paths lead to this stereotype more than others; we'll still learn that no matter what you choose to do in the sports industry, being a "nice guy" will help you finish first!

CHAPTER 2

The Science of Generosity

———

In the world of sports, competitiveness is baked right in. And for some reason, competitiveness is synonymous with doing whatever it takes to get to the top, regardless of how it makes others feel or what you need to do to them. Through research, much smarter people than myself have found that not to be completely true, and may even be the opposite.

Being competitive is not the problem, people can be competitive and respect each other as fellow humans on planet Earth. But when we think of the business world, all bets are off and thrown out the window. The common phrase of "nice guys finish last" seems to ring true with so many people when we really only see this happen in the movies. Outside of some anecdotal stories that you might have heard from someone who heard it from someone else, how often do the nice guys really finish last? And how often are the bad guys really finishing first? Yes, there is no debate that we can look at some very prominent people in very high positions and know enough bad stories about them and how they got there.

But there are so many other really great people that have done just as much good. That's where I want to focus my time, energy, and effort. I'm a believer in doing the right thing not because it's easy or because good things happen to good people (like my mom always ironically says), but because it's the right thing to do. I believe in karma and that good things *do* happen to good people.

Adam Grant, the youngest full-time professor at the Wharton School, has something to say about if being a good person gives you a better chance at finishing first. Let's start with some of his basics. There are three types of people when it comes to preferences of reciprocity: givers, takers, and matchers. Takers want to get more than they give, givers like to give more than they get, and matchers want an equal balance of giving and getting. It has been found that in workplaces, most people are matchers. You do or did this for me so I'll do this for you, and vice versa.[10]

You would think that givers would be nice people that do well sometimes because eventually someone would give something back. You might also assume that takers will always come out on top because they are always taking what they want. Grant poses other obstacles on why none of that may be true. Engineers that are givers are less productive and effective, and medical students that are givers are less productive at first. In the end, med school students end up being the best at giving once all is said and done. Another positive comes from salespeople; they are normally better performers as givers, about

10 Grant, Adam M. Give and Take: A Revolutionary Approach to Success. New York, N.Y.: Viking. 2013.

twenty-five percent better at selling than matchers or takers. "Being a giver is not good for a hundred-yard dash, but it's valuable in a marathon."[11] By doing this over and over again, in certain situations, you'll end up ahead as a giver in the long run, even if it does take a while! Business isn't a zero-sum game, and it's not a sprint either!

"This is what I find most magnetic about successful givers: they get to the top without cutting others down, finding ways of expanding the pie that benefit themselves and the people around them. Whereas success is zero-sum in a group of takers, in groups of givers, it may be true that the whole is greater than the sum of the parts."[12] Considering the abundance in the world, takers are more likely to be trying this in a zero-sum game rather than one that is nearly infinite. Takers succeed at someone else's expense while givers spread their success further, allowing others to partake in it. And when we take into account social media and the speed of a message, it's hard to hide from something bad you did or have done.

With sports and the sports industry being much more male-dominated, it's understandable that the machismo we discuss in the previous chapter could rear its head into more situations within this giver and taker world as well. "The fear of being judged as weak or naive prevents many people from operating like givers at work." Grant makes the point that at work many people will be takers as a sign to show others that they aren't weak, which can again be affected by the already competitive nature of the sports business industry. [13]

11 Ibid.

12 Ibid.

13 Ibid.

So, it sounds like it would be easy, just give as much as you can so others give back, right? Wrong! If you give so you can succeed it doesn't quite work the same. You need to want to give because it's the right thing to do, not because you're expecting something in return. In reality, you're essentially a taker, or at least a matcher at that point.

Considering how long I've been in the sports business world, a little over two years now, I still struggle with this from time to time. I'm a huge believer in karma, so I look to give in as many situations as possible! Sometimes, though, I give without asking for anything in return. While I'm okay with this, you will hear later on in this book from David Meltzer, former CEO of Leigh Steinberg, you need to make sure you are also asking for help. [14]

If you can clearly lay out how someone can help you, they are more likely to help you! Sounds like rocket science, I know, but it also is very important to understand. Asking for help in general, or asking to help in general, can actually be frustrating from your counterparts' points of view. Not being specific can make things much more difficult for them than if you just asked for their help in a specific way. This is something that I'm still working on everyday and doing my best to get better at! Adam Grant agrees, "Regardless of their reciprocity styles, people love to be asked for advice." [15] Most people on this planet want to help; giving them the opportunity to help you is something that most would jump at!

Learning the give-and-take nature of the business world is crucial to becoming successful. While I wouldn't call

14 Ibid.
15 Ibid.

myself successful yet, I can see the future looking bright. By being a giver, I have had the amazing opportunity to connect with more people.

I have also seen this give and take specifically when writing this book! I was looking for high-profile people in the sports business world, understanding that their time is very valuable to them. But just by asking them to be a part of this book, they were more than happy to give their time, knowing this could be something that helps many people moving forward. Now, obviously, not everyone was able to help, but it seemed that the ones that did have a break somewhere in their life that they could attribute to someone else. Giving me their time, energy, and effort can be something that will bring them some sort of return, whether intrinsically or potentially for business down the road!

Throughout this book you will find the stories of many great women and men that show how they were able to succeed in their careers. Within those stories you will see the points where they did what was necessary by adding value to others, doing whatever was necessary, sacrificing their time, and more. These people are truly givers and they have been able to master being good people, which in turn has helped them become even more successful. Heck, they were all nice enough to allow me to interview them so I could learn their stories better and share them with you!

A few more points on givers and takers to hopefully make you more of a giver than a taker: "Takers are selfish, failed givers are selfless, and successful givers are otherish (they care about others, but also have ambitious goals for themselves). Selflessness becomes overwhelming. Otherishness means giving more than you get, but still keeping your interests in sight. How is this different from matchers? Matchers expect something back from everyone they help. Otherish givers give with no strings attached, but are careful not to overextend themselves."[16] Being self-aware is a superpower in my opinion, and understanding where you fall into these categories can really help you get better at business!

Just because you're giving doesn't mean it will work, and it doesn't mean you'll get tired of it. You have to remember that you have goals and aspirations too! Asking for help is never a problem, in fact, it's encouraged (as you'll read later). Give because you want to, but if there is something you think you can be helped with, make sure to ask so you can get further ahead and help even more people!

---

16 Ibid.

PART 2

CHAPTER 3

Adding Value

———

"The easiest way to enter sports, 'where's my point of entry,' is to provide value, meaning, the bottom line."

DAVID MELTZER

GIVE BEFORE YOU GET

When you meet a rich, successful person in the world of sports, what's the first thing you think? Some that come to mind: "They're so lucky," "I can do that," "Maybe she can help me," "I wonder if he'll introduce me."

First, I don't believe in luck, so throw that one out. Of course, you can probably do that, so why don't you? Get to it! She probably can help you, but why should she? Absolutely he can introduce you, but what's in it for him?

Most of these thoughts are ether projecting, making you inferior, jealousy, or creating expectations that another person should be helping you. All of them are possible, but with that mindset, none of it will come true.

Through the many conversations I've had over the course of writing this book, one of the main topics that has been touched on is adding value to others. *But* you can't have the expectation that anything will come back in return.

We spoke earlier about Mark Simon and how he was able to break into the sports industry through an opportunity that he didn't expect much in return from. He was able to utilize the relationship created later on to get his "dream job" at ESPN.

Mark Simon is a senior research analyst at Sports Info Solutions, the leader in the collection, analysis, and delivery of top-quality sports data content, but he is most likely best-known for his work on ESPN for over fifteen years. During his time at ESPN, Mark rose from research assistant to lead researcher where he oversaw all the baseball content put out by ESPN's research group. He even ran the ESPN Stats and Info Twitter feed from its infancy to well over one million followers. And to top it all off, he wrote a book while he was there too!

It may seem like Mark was destined to work at ESPN and have a big role while he was there, but that wasn't always the case. Mark had to start at the bottom just like many of the other people you will read about in this book, and there is nothing wrong with starting at the bottom, there are actually more positives that come from it than negatives.

While attending The College of New Jersey in Ewing, New Jersey (formerly Trenton State, but that's a whole other book in itself), Mark was majoring in Journalism and always wanted the opportunity to work in sports. He became a part of the radio station there and befriended the two professors that worked in the department. With so few people in the department, this allowed Mark to get more one-on-one time with the teachers and department heads that could help him get a better grasp on the industry and what it takes to win. One of his professors had a lot of contacts at *The Trenton Times* which helped him to get his first job there during college. "*The Trenton Times* had an opening for an internship for the first time in many years, and the professor kinda pushed me along to kinda get me in." It was part-time work, but it allowed him to learn more and more about journalism and covering sports while still young enough to be molded.

In an interesting twist, Trenton, New Jersey, one of the smallest media markets in America, played a huge role in Mark's career advancement. "The way that Trenton was unique was that Trenton, New Jersey, is a mid-sized city but it has two newspapers. It was at the time one of the smaller two paper markets in the country." *The Trenton Times'* rival newspaper had an owner who loved the sport of hockey more than any other, so when Trenton got its first minor league hockey team, the Trenton Titans, the rival newspaper covered the team as if every day was the Stanley Cup Finals. "He had decided that his beat writer would travel to all the games and they were going to cover it like they were a tabloid with huge headlines."

This led to an arms race of sorts, with *The Trenton Times* needing to keep up and cover the team in the same way, and they thought Mark was the man for the job! "And so, our response to that was: me! I got to be super gung-ho and super enthusiastic. I had a once-a-week column where I had trade rumors that coaches told me and I would get to pontificate about all the weird stuff that we would see." He was thrusted into a beat writer role for this minor league hockey team that he would not have been able to get anywhere else, especially this soon out of college.

Unfortunately, Mark was never offered a full-time position at *The Trenton Times*, so this got him thinking about "dream job" scenarios and what he would do if he could. Growing up in the 1990s and 2000s, Mark was naturally a big fan of ESPN, the self-proclaimed worldwide leader in sports. This led him to consider what he could do at ESPN and how he could go about finding a job there.

"In August of 2001, the Mariners blew a 12-0 lead to the Indians. I had been reading Jayson Stark on ESPN.com for a while and he had a column called "Useless Information," where he would talk about silly pieces of trivia that happened in games. I thought about it and I said 'I've got the perfect thing for Jayson Stark."

Mark decided to take a shot and send a letter to a higher-up at ESPN to create a relationship. He wasn't asking for anything, though, he was trying to give! He was trying to be of service, trying to add value by understanding what Jayson Stark does and his sense of humor. Understanding how you can help someone and showing them that you care can take you a very long way, but you have to pay attention! "Dear Jayson Stark, this is the biggest lead blown in a baseball game since Charlie Brown came on in relief for Peppermint Patty in the bottom of the ninth with two outs and the team up 50-0, and gave up fifty-one runs to lose the game."

This funny little anecdote became a huge piece of Mark's career. Just a cute little story he decided to write to someone at ESPN for fun helped catapult his career. "Jayson Stark read it and used it!" How cool is that? Getting to see your name on ESPN.com with a writer that you really enjoy couldn't be much better.

Being a huge sports fan and journalist at that, having a job at ESPN was a dream for Mark. Doing anything at the Worldwide Leader in Sports would be the best way to fully kick off his career, so he started to apply. "I had applied as a college basketball temp at ESPN in 1997 (it was a researcher position) so I knew that there was a researcher job available for everything. So, I was like, 'There's got to be something for *Baseball Tonight*, that's my kind of job.'" With baseball being his favorite sport, he wanted to at least try and do something in that field. "I hated applying to jobs at big companies because you send your resume to human resources and it would get lost."

While we think the sports business industry is big, once you start meeting people you realize how quickly you become only a few degrees away from everybody! Knowing how to take advantage of this is something to learn in any industry, but here we'll keep it to sports. ESPN Inc. operates as a subsidiary of The Walt Disney Company. Based in Bristol, Connecticut, ESPN has approximately four thousand employees (approximately eight thousand worldwide). With numbers this big, we can only assume how many resumes are sent every day to ESPN for sports-hungry fans looking for a job. And while these numbers were most likely smaller in the late '90s, Mark still understood he needed to stand out and speak with someone rather than throw his name into a lottery ball machine. [17]

Mark then realized that he did have one person's email address at the company, and that person worked specifically in baseball! Learning how to ask for help, especially in an industry as big and top-heavy as the sports world, can really jump-start any endeavor you're looking to accomplish. So, Mark reached out to Jayson and asked for some help! "Dear Jayson Stark, you don't know me, I don't know you. I'm not looking for a reference, I'm looking for a name. Who is the person who does the hiring for *Baseball Tonight*?" Unfortunately, Jayson directed Mark to an ESPN producer named Judson Burch, who would later work with Mark, but was not the person making hiring decisions. By total luck, Judson replied to Mark with the name of his future boss, Craig Wachs! He made enough of an impression that he was then introduced to the correct person through someone he'd never met before! "I always tell people this: strike when the opportunity is there, don't be shy about reaching out, there's gotta be a bit of luck involved, but bet on yourself, too, certainly."

ALWAYS MAKE SURE TO PROVIDE VALUE, NO MATTER WHAT

As we see in Mark's story, he was able to provide value to Jayson Stark through a funny story that he could utilize for his job. This made Jayson's life easier and made his readers happier. When Mark provided the funny anecdote, it was not under the assumption that Jayson would provide Mark with a name, nor did he expect to get a job out of it.

17 "ESPN Careers & Jobs," Zippia, accessed September 9, 2020.

By going about your career in this sense, and your life for that matter, you will be able to create more authentic relationships and people will want to give back to you! (The Law of Reciprocity.)

We can move from journalism to sports medicine to see the same theme at work. Dr. Meeta Singh is a board-certified physician focused on the applied science of sleep. Considering humans spend about one-third of their lives asleep, it makes sense that there are incredible people like Dr. Singh out there studying how it works, and how we can do it better. Dr. Singh has two different American Board of Psychiatry and Neurology certifications, one for psychiatry and one for sleep medicine. She earned her education at Government Medical College, Chandigarh, in India, graduated in 1997, and she then went on to the Mayo Clinic for her residency and internships for psychiatry ending in 2004. In 2005, she made her way to the Henry Ford Hospital for her fellowship in sleep medicine.

Dr. Singh is absolutely fascinated by sleep. "If you think about it, why are we asleep? You're not responding to the environment you're in, absolutely not doing anything, you're vulnerable. So, if there are any predators or if there was any danger, you'd be completely vulnerable. So, if sleep was not serving an absolutely central function, it would totally be a horrible, colossal waste of time, a huge mistake on the part of evolution." She was so interested that she decided she wanted to dedicate her life's work to understanding more about it and helping other become better at it by exercising their "sleep muscle."

While working as the medical director at the Henry Ford Sleep Laboratory in Detroit, Michigan, she originally started to work with CEOs from the car manufacturing companies in the area to help them when they were traveling across the country and overseas to negotiate deals. "I was doing a lot of work in helping with jet lag and poor sleep with the auto executives, especially when they would travel to Asia, or they would have to wake up early in the morning or late at night to do these meetings. I was trying to help them with sleep optimization." Considering the amount of money on the line for these automakers, it stands to reason that they would want to be in tip-top shape when discussing multi-million or multi-billion-dollar deals.

After doing this for a little while, Dr. Singh "fell" into sports by providing value for the local NFL team, the Detroit Lions. She overheard an interview with a so-called sleep expert about the nonsense he was spewing to her hometown team. "It wasn't based on anything, he really wasn't a true expert, it was just, you know, complete rubbish." Hearing the content of what this person was saying and how wrong he was, Dr. Singh couldn't stand for poor information going out into the world about a topic she cared so deeply for. So, she decided to take actions into her own hands and make sure that the people received the correct information. "I called Dr. Michael Workings who is the team doctor for the... Lions here... and I said, 'Whoever you had speaking to you guys, you know, doesn't make sense.'"

It was an easy outreach for Dr. Singh to make considering her in-depth knowledge of the subject and wanting to provide the correct information and as much value as she can. It also helps that Dr. Workings works through the

Henry Ford Health Systems, the same one as Dr. Singh, but he works directly with sports medicine. Considering how easy it must have been for Dr. Workings to see Dr. Singh's credentials and expertise, it made sense he would ask her to come in and help the team out! "He turned around and said, 'Well why don't you come and give us a talk then.'"

Dr. Singh is now one of the most well-known sleep doctors in all of sports, all because she knew a lot about her field and didn't want someone spouting off incorrect information about something she loved so much. This is just another of the countless examples of how in the sports world, people will be able to get ahead by providing significant value to others because it's the right thing to do, *not* because they want something back in return. Ironically, these all land with huge returns though.

Providing value to others has been something that I was taught immediately in my professional career, but the "no expectations" part was something I learned within the last two years. It has completely changed the way that I view people and sports business. By always looking to help others and find ways to add to what they are already doing, I've found many more relationships come back my way. When I go about introducing someone, having them on a podcast, or providing feedback or advice for them, I never expect them to give me anything back. I do it because I believe doing good is always the right thing to do and sometimes it results in positive consequences, but even if it doesn't, I will still continue to do it.

One way that has provided returns for me in the form of exciting opportunities is by allowing me to co-host a show on *SiriusXM Radio*. I had my friend Jason Mezrahi from *Win Daily Sports* on my podcast, *For the Love of Sports*, at the very beginning because I liked his story and what *Win Daily Sports* was all about. We met over a year before the formal interview and would run into each other on almost a monthly basis. When I asked him to be on the show, he said yes and we scheduled an interview right out of the gate.

It was publicity for him, small but better than nothing, and it allowed him to share his story and his business with a new audience. Doesn't hurt! This was an easy value to provide from my side, but before, during, and after, I did not expect too much to come from it. He enjoyed the interview, we got to chatting and I learned that his current co-host of the *SiriusXM Radio* show was no longer able to do it because he recently had a baby and the timing of the show made it difficult for him to do.

Just as I don't believe in luck, I don't believe in coincidences either. Working hard and putting yourself in the best position go hand in hand. We will touch upon this later in the book. Jason enjoyed our conversation; I know a lot about sports, showed initiative, and he needed help. This turned out to be a great opportunity for the two of us.

I provided a small value to him which he appreciated, and in return he allowed me to help him and be on an internationally broadcasted radio show that millions of people hear. I'd say it was worth the hour-long interview for the two of us.

YOU + X = SUCCESS

Throughout your life, I challenge you to look back and see how the dots have been connected for you to get to where you are. You'd be surprised at how many things you can trace back to long before the opportunity was ever a thought in your head.

What I have found is these opportunities start happening quicker if you start adding value to others along the way of your life. One thing truly leads to another, which leads to another, and another. The people you meet and places you go will become more enjoyable if you give yourself to others while you're with them. You'll never really know what is possible until you watch the acceleration of your career and, more importantly, your life while you are giving without the expectation of anything in return.

CHAPTER 4

Fun/Free Work to Getting Well-Paid

———

I was watching the UFC and saw the very famous Joe Rogan as the commentator and I asked myself, "How did Joe Rogan become the color commentator for the UFC?" As I was traveling down the rabbit hole of *The Joe Rogan Experience Podcast* and articles written about him, I started to realize this wasn't as odd of a story as I once thought, at least from the perspective of how he got the job; doing what you love can lead to a career in sports.

Fighting has always been something Joe Rogan was interested in. He started engaging in the sport through karate when he was fourteen years old. By fifteen, he already received his black belt within taekwondo. Joe was even shooting to make it to the Olympic team for a short period of time! His knowledge of fighting is mixed, to say the least, with training within wrestling, Brazilian jiu-jitsu, muay Thai, and kickboxing as well.

We all knew him as the "*Fear Factor* Guy" because this was easily his biggest gig within the public eye, starting his public accent with the show in 2001. For anyone that doesn't know *Fear Factor* or has never seen the version with Joe Rogan on it, the early 2000s were a very weird time. For three years, the show was an absolute hit. 2001 through 2004, the show was routinely one of the most popular shows on television. Joe's first time ever on the "sidelines" of a UFC match actually came in 1997 at UFC 12 in Atlanta, a few years before he even got the *Fear Factor* gig. He had no idea what he was doing and even recalls them throwing him directly into the fire with no formal training. "It just was a position that was available. The UFC was very small back then, very few people knew what it was. They needed someone to do post-fight interviews." [18] Rogan did these gigs for a short period of time with no knowledge of what sideline reporters were supposed to do; it was more just something to pass the time. The UFC was eventually sold and Rogan left the gig for actual paying jobs within comedy and eventually *Fear Factor*. "I was actually losing money. I would make more money doing a weekend at a comedy club than I would doing the UFC. And it just got to a point where it was just too much of a pain in the ass. So, I still remained a fan, but I backed away."[19]

Joe continued to go to the shows and enjoy himself with friends, but the new ownership wanted someone to help be a notable figure in the space of mixed martial arts (MMA) to help spread the word and amplify the sport.

18 Jon Fuentes, "Joe Rogan Reveals How He Became The Voice Of UFC," MMA News, February 6, 2019.

19 Ibid.

The new owner and commissioner, Dana White, asked Joe to come back on as a commentator, but was quickly rejected. He eventually wore Rogan down like a river through bedrock. "'I don't want to do commentary, man. I'm here to get drunk and watch people kick the shit out of each other. I'm not here to work.' And he talked me into it for one show. UFC 37.5."[20]

This then quickly turned into something that happened more than once or twice. "I did that, and the rest was history. I did like twelve of them for free. The UFC didn't have any money. They were hemorrhaging money. There were rich people that owned it, but it was not a profitable venture. And I said, 'Look, just get me there, get me and my friends tickets, and I'll do it.' And that's how I operated for over a year, and then I just became 'The Commentator.' It's just weird."[21] The perks seemed to be good enough to continue the joy of the sport!

The UFC was bought for four billion dollars in 2016 by Endeavor, a media and marketing global leader in sports, entertainment, and fashion, (and speculated to be worth more than seven billion dollars by their bombastic president Dana White) and Joe is handsomely paid to be the play-by-play commentator.[22] This got me thinking, how often does this happen in life and in the sports industry? Turns out a lot, and it even has happened to me! I then started to look at the sports industry, as well as others, to see where this happened to people we either know and

---

20   Ibid.

21   Ibid.

22   Trent Reinsmith, "With Dana White's Claim That The UFC Is Worth $7 Billion, It's Time To Revisit Fighter Pay," Forbes, Aug 21, 2018.

love today or who are friends of mine that have turned something fun they liked to do into careers.

A great story I always look to as inspiration on why doing free work can be the best thing for your career is looking at David Rock, known as DRock (pronounced dee-rock), who works with Gary Vaynerchuk. Gary is a marketing genius who will one day own the New York Jets and currently owns a sports agency that his brother AJ runs. Gary Vee, as he is commonly known, was born in Russia before his parents brought him over here to the United States. They settled in New Jersey where his father did whatever he needed to ensure his family could get by. By a very young age, Gary was working in his father's wine store located in Springfield, New Jersey.

Gary has always been ahead of the curve when it came to new ways to market his products and services. He started his YouTube page before everyone else had one where he would review wine and utilize this as a sales tool for his father's store. This taught Gary that video content was the "next big thing," which he decided to utilize in another fashion. Gary realized filming the everyday aspects of his life brought him many more followers and ambassadors than the normal, run-of-the-mill marketing efforts. By capturing not just the good, but the bad of his day, it made him much more relatable to everyone else on the Internet. His big personality and intense nature also made him a hit. His main sidekick, known to many that follow him, is DRock, his videographer.

DRock got his first camera at fourteen and eventually graduated from Columbia University in New York City, the best place to find people and stories. It took him a while to find a job and he did literally anything he could to upgrade his portfolio. He slept on his sister's couch for over five years to save money and got creative on how he could utilize his time and energy to be the best he could. "At first, I slept in my sister and brother-in-law's basement and would commute to the city in their car and sit in Starbucks and order coffee and a banana and literally post ads on Craigslist and responded to all and any posts that had to do with film, movie production, editing, etcetera. I made restaurant videos for twenty dollars (plus a meal)." He learned how to be resourceful and learned even more about his craft doing as much as he could in a short period of time. "This went on for five years and I would do it all over again and double down on the free work. We have way more opportunity as creators now to build awareness and market ourselves, just gotta be humble and put in the work." Then came his big break.

"January 2014 at Columbia University was the first time I heard Gary speak. He told so many truths and his genuineness was refreshing, even the way he dressed was unapologetic (a Deckhead sweater, jeans with no belt, a ball cap, and Nikes)."

He reached out to Gary because, if anyone out there has heard him speak, he always encourages people to reach out. No response. DRock saw another post from Gary, telling his fans to reach out. Still no response. Not just sitting on his thumbs, DRock stayed working and creating. A few weeks later, the wait was finally over and Gary said he'd be interested in having DRock do *more free work* for him, if he was interested. Gary, at this time, was a multi-millionaire, but DRock rolled with it. He created a project called "Clouds and Dirt" where he followed Gary around for a day and created a type of "day in the life" video that has been viewed over 184,000 times on YouTube alone. The creation of this one video led to Gary hiring DRock and, for the last five years, he has been following him around recording all the days in his life to show people how far you can come when you pay attention to the things that matter. "Now we're planning on taking over the world, one video at a time." [23]

Let's look at two more examples of people in sports doing things for fun and eventually getting paid to do them. A friend of mine, Marc Luino, or GiraffeNeckMarc to his YouTube community, started a YouTube page for fun because he saw another famous YouTuber create a FIFA video that allowed him the opportunity to travel around the world to watch and play the game he loved.[24] It allowed him to learn and understand how the space worked without "being too professional." In college, he needed to satiate his baseball fix because he was no longer playing the sport. "I ended up making up a You-Tube channel. Never was it the plan for it to be my job, never was it to be a full thing, and I caught the bug and I'm addicted."

Marc continued to master his craft over time and has now accumulated over 160,000 subscribers as of September 2020. He does what he loves, talk about baseball, and gets paid through the monetization of his YouTube page

23 David 'DRock' Rock, "How I Got My Job For Gary Vaynerchuk," Medium, Jun 1, 2017.

24 Marc Luino, "Giraffe Neck Marc," accessed Mar 25, 2015, YouTube Channel.

by putting out quality content that people enjoy. His page went through a few iterations, but he found what people were interested in; he noticed there weren't many daily baseball YouTubers, and he went for it. The opportunity to become full-time was during his last semester at college; "make videos people want to watch" was some of the best advice he received when he was starting to create more and more content. "I hit my stride my last month of classes, which was interesting because last month of classes you have your finals and you don't want to screw up, so I was juggling that along with putting out these videos now, because once you hit that wave in YouTube, you have to ride it for as long as possible." Marc understood not only how to create content, but what to create, the medium he was using, and how to take advantage of it. This works for each medium you can create content for; most people just don't take the time to learn! By putting the time and energy into something he thoroughly enjoyed, he will hopefully be able to continue to create content for his own page, or even be paid by a major organization to create for them. Marc has been able to create a sustainable income for himself through YouTube and sponsorship of his videos. It's enough that he does not need a full-time or even part-time job to keep him afloat, and he can love what he does every day.

A more well-known example of doing something you love out of enjoyment and eventually getting paid to do it would be Mike Florio, the creator of the famous site ProFootballTalk.com. Mike started at a little-known media site that was eventually bought by ESPN.com, and he spent about six months writing for the mothership.

He left ESPN around 2001. He was practicing labor law in Clarksburg, West Virginia, a small city of about 16,500 people that attracted industry and manufacturing businesses. While there, he started ProFootballTalk.com as another outlet to speak his mind about the NFL in the early 2000s. After some time, his website blew up, attracting significant eyeballs to his page on a weekly basis.

After about eight years, it was announced that ProFootballTalk would become an affiliate of NBC. Mike Florio is now looked at as a preeminent figure in the sports media landscape, hosting a morning talk show that is simulcasted to the NBC Sports television channel. [25]

The opportunities within sports are far and wide, but one sure-fire way to build a portfolio of work is to do some of it for free, as many have before you and many will after. Always make sure to look out for the scams, but if there's something you love to do, do it! As for myself, I started a podcast, *For the Love of Sports*, for fun that goes along with this book (you can find it wherever you listen to your favorite shows) that has already paid dividends.

One of my first episodes was with my friend Jason Mezrahi who owns *Win Daily*, a media company that is based around daily fantasy sports and sports betting. Jason had a co-host on his *SiriusXM* show that had to drop out because he recently had a baby, which allowed our interview about his story to turn into an interview for a co-host spot on an internationally broadcasted radio show without me even knowing. I jumped at the opportunity to do the show and can be another example of

---

25 Sam Farmer, "Profootballtalk.com acquired by NBC," *LA Times*, June 15, 2009.

doing what you love for fun, doing whatever you can to get better at it, and then reaping the rewards that come with your newfound skills, knowledge, and desire!

Jason was far from my first interview; at that point, I already had close to 150 under my belt. He could tell that I was already comfortable in front of a microphone and knew if he asked, it wasn't going to be something scary for me to deal with. He also knew that I would put in the work because, outside of the 150 plus shows that I've already done, I was also running my business for almost two years and was looking for more ways to expand. It takes a while for everything to add up, but if there is something you love and you're willing to do it for free and put in the work to get better, just keep going and one day you can make it too!

BE AWARE OF BEING TAKEN ADVANTAGE OF

Obviously, not all stories are like the ones I have highlighted in the previous section. For each of these, there may be a thousand that don't end in glory. One example of the many are writers for sites that are promising much more than they are giving. Many times in sports, you are told you need to build your resume. You have to accumulate something for people to see before you get paid to do it at all, especially in the high-demand and high-supply industry of sports. I think it's a great idea to understand more about this from someone who has worked for one of these sites that promises to be a premiere resume-builder. I also think it depends on what you're looking to get out of something like this. Are you looking for something fun to do, as we spoke about previously, or are you looking for a professional career in sports media?

Nathan Graber-Lipperman wrote for a "do it yourself" or "by and for fan" website that would have young up-and-comers in the industry create content for them for little to no money as a way to add to their resumes. "From my personal experience, I became a writer for (fan-run website) with quite explicit guidelines. I was not going to receive any form of monetary compensation, a point I agreed to before signing up." Knowing what you're getting into is very important, but anyway you can utilize what you're doing for the future is a good thing! "[Fan-run website] opened a whole lot of doors, operating as a great resume-builder while lending a superb look into the media world. I've even formed connections with people not only across the nation, but all over the world, a vital facet of the industry I one day hope to partake in."

Not everyone is in the same boat when it comes to this story with Nathan, as well as the ones I highlighted previously about many others who were able to find their dream jobs out of their passion. Many people do get taken advantage of and it can be harmful to their careers. Nathan was able to see how this opportunity could lead to others that would allow him to do this full-time. "The extremely positive response I received from my first couple of posts on [the site] influenced me a great deal, though, pushing me toward some form of journalism before I eventually settled on a track that strives to combine business and media."

These sites have their place in the sports media landscape and the career arch of many people. Understanding where that is within your life is important and can lead to many great things, or potentially hard times depending on your mindset.

CHAPTER 5

Hard Work

———

KAY ADAMS NEVER STOPS

Kay Adams isn't here to listen to why you *can't* do it. Being born to immigrant parents from Poland, Kay was told from a young age that she would pretty much have to do this thing called life on her own. "My parents grew up in Poland and immigrated over here and had a crazy work ethic," Adams says. "It was 'work as hard as you can and we can't afford to pay for college, so you're gonna have to get a scholarship's mentality. Once I was on my own, I had to pay for school." Growing up in the Windy City and needing to grit her teeth, Kay learned if she outworked others, it would bring her further than sheer talent alone. [26]

After graduating high school, Kay attended the University of Missouri where she did whatever was necessary to make money and get by. She initially wanted to get into journalism, but after taking some time, she realized she wanted to do more editorial type work. She was looking

---

26 Jeff Eisenband, "Bartending, Country Music and Kay Adams' Relentless Path to Success," Front Office Sports, February 1, 2019.

for a job at a radio station to fulfill this new urge she had and did what she needed to do to get whatever job they'd give her. "I knocked on a woman's door and I said, 'Do you have any spots open?' She said, 'We have a country radio music spot open from midnight to 6:00 a.m., Fridays and Saturdays. Do you want it? Do you like country music?' I couldn't even say honky-tonk, but I was like, 'Sure, I'll do it.'" How badly do you want it if you say no? [27]

When you do take that 12:00 a.m. to 6:00 a.m. job, you should make sure you talk to everybody; you never know who you'll meet in the break room at 3:00 a.m. "I'd go to get coffee and the ESPN guys who had the radio station next door, we'd talk about the St. Louis Rams and the Kansas City Chiefs and they'd invite me at two in the morning to come in and talk sports." And that is how dreams are made. After working ridiculous hours and putting herself in uncomfortable situations, she is clearly on her way. [28]

With her love for discussing sports, she decided that diving deeper into sports was something that could help her long-term in this potential career path. Being in St. Louis, she went knocking on more doors and landed at the St. Louis Cardinals facility where she asked them to do jobs for next to nothing just to gain the experience, knowledge, and connections she knew she would need. "I wanted to work for pennies, for peanuts. The Cardinals basically paid me in beer to be there for seven-hour rain delays." Working for free means you have to do something else to make enough money to get by, so Kay took

27 Ibid.
28 Ibid.

up a job as a bartender to pay the bills and continue to talk sports with anyone who was interested at Willie's Pub and Pool in Columbia. [29]

Knowing where Kay came from lends us a glimpse into what she had growing up, and it wasn't money, but the work ethic of someone who knew they could win with one more rep than the next person. "My advice is there's not really an excuse because there's not really a thing where if you have money, you're gonna make it, and it's not a thing where you need to have all the talent. I know that I'll make it if I outwork the person to my left and my right." She was willing to do more than anyone else now and then, and she got to where she is because of it. Most people wouldn't work two jobs, most people wouldn't work for free, but most people aren't Kay Adams. [30]

Then came another great opportunity that Kay got the chance to take because of the smart decisions she made in the past. "*SiriusXM* was launching their fantasy sports station. I launched the station with them from St. Louis. I had an ISDN box that I would plug into and I was part of a show, as they were looking to cast a female talent to be part of their show." Since Kay spoke with the gentleman in the break room at 3:00 a.m. and got on their ESPN show, she could say she had ample experience for the job. For as hard as Kay has worked throughout her career, the deck has been stacked against women within the sports broadcasting industry. "As of 2014, ninety percent of editorial roles, ninety percent of assistant editorial roles, eighty-eight percent of columnists, eighty-seven

29 Ibid.

30 Ibid.

percent of reporters, and ninety-five percent of anchors are men. Of the 183 sport talk shows, there are only two female hosts." [31]

Kay's hard work has clearly paid off because she has risen to one of the most well-known television personalities for the NFL Network as the host of *Good Morning Football*, the three-hour morning show that discusses football five days a week all year long. Kay has also used her knowledge and experience on *FantasyZone*, the Sunday football show that airs during the season that talks about what's happening in the fantasy football world. This is even more impressive when you look at the landscape of the NFL Network and sports as a whole. "Since its launch in November 2003, only 12 percent of the NFL Network's sixty-two analysts, reporters, announcers, and hosts have been women." Being one of the twelve impressive women that have gotten to heights normally given to men, this does not stop Kay from looking for outside positions as well. She currently works on DAZN's boxing coverage to help bring a female perspective to the fighting games. [32]

If there is something we all can learn from Kay, whether you're trying to break into the sports world or just trying to get better at your current job, it is to literally outwork everyone else. It's easy to say just work hard and things will happen, but what do you consider working hard? Is it "if you want to break into editorial sports content you'll take the 12:00 a.m. shift at the country music station"

31 Daniel Paramo, "Gender inequality in sports broadcasting apparent to viewers," The Daily Evergreen, October 5, 2017.

32 Jeff Eisenband, "Bartending, Country Music and Kay Adams' Relentless Path to Success," Front Office Sports, February 1, 2019.

hard? Is it "work for practically free so you need another job working as a bartender" hard? If not, maybe your definition of "hard" needs to change to something more similar to Kay's, because she did it and is still not stopping. "Outwork everyone; take any job. Take the country radio music station job from 12:00 to 6:00 a.m. Don't turn down the internship. Go for that too. Diversify as much as you can." [33]

HARD WORK CONTINUES TO PAY OFF

Sounds kind of silly, don't they? Those quotes from the beginning of the chapter? Yes, they are. "Hustle Porn" has become very big on the Internet as of the time of writing this. "This idea that unless you are suffering, grinding, and working every hour of every day, you're not working hard enough." [34]

This type of social media makes it seem like if you're not waking up at 4:30 a.m. and going to sleep at 12:00 a.m., working every minute of the day, you're not working hard enough. Yes, ridiculous. But working hard actually is something you're going to want to do.

The supply and demand of the sports industry are both very high. The jobs are extremely coveted (demand), and there are a lot of people willing to do whatever it takes to get them (supply). This will make it very hard to get a job you want unless you're willing to go above and beyond. Unfortunately, many employers are aware of this and will take advantage; more on that later. Understanding that

---

33 Ibid.

34 Carlos Hildalgo, "I used to believe in hustle porn, and now I think it's the antithesis of the American Dream," Fast Company, June 20, 2019.

there is inherent risk in doing some free or fun work is still almost a necessity.

A lot of people are against non-paid internships, but in the sports world, it's that or way, way, way too much work for little pay. You need to gain some ability and experience, and if you're not going to do it on your own, do some work for free, or overwork yourself to the bone, you probably won't get it. If there are people willing to do more than you are at a lesser rate, because they know that in a few years they will have networked with the best of them and gained valuable experience they can point to, then why would anyone hire you?

Kay Adams went the route of working herself to the bone for a small amount of money to get all the opportunities she has to this point. She has absolutely earned all the money and fame from those opportunities. She understood that money in the beginning doesn't really matter as long as you can pay your bills and buy things that bring you even closer to your goal!

Now, I do not have the job I dream of when I open my eyes each morning, but I'm willing to do whatever is necessary to get there! In my wildest dreams, I would want to interview people for a living, and help share their stories, experiences, and wisdom with the world through conversation so people can learn and be better. All of that within the world of sports. I would love to speak in front of crowds to help spread the knowledge that I have learned far and wide from some of the sports industry's best and brightest minds, much like I'm trying in this book!

So, if I want to get paid to do something, I need to do it for free (or very little pay)! But I've done it on my own with a lot of hard work in finding people, booking times, staying up late, getting up early, and doing whatever necessary to develop my skills, knowledge, and desire for what I want. More on skills, knowledge, and desire later.

Understanding the direction in which I want to go gives me a clear idea of who I should talk to and learn from. This keeps my eyes downfield on the prize of being the happiest person on planet Earth. True story.

The reason I love sharing people's stories so much is because that was a pillar I started my business on. I work with Olympic athletes to help them with sponsorships and partnerships. But I needed a way to find all of these incredible athletes. So, I started a podcast, just like everyone else in 2019 and 2020. I reached out with a reason, "I want to help spread your (amazing) story to the world," and started to create relationships with some of the coolest people I know with the best stories around. The more I did this, the more I realized I have the knack for it, and the more I absolutely loved it! This led to creating another podcast so I could talk to anyone in the sports world, and another realization that if that was my full-time job, I'd be the happiest person in the world.

Let's see a similar path in the next story to another famous NFL personality!

IAN RAPOPORT JUST KEEPS GOING

Career paths are funny things. As many before me have said, "Want to make God laugh? Have a plan." The reason

I say this is because when you're young and fresh out of college, most people have an idea of what they want to do and why they want to do it without much experience in the field. Our NFL insider king Ian Rapoport is no different. I mean, who leaves college wanting to become an insider to any of the major sports?

As a fan of fantasy football, or even the real thing, Ian Rapoport is someone you probably know and love, but I'm sure you didn't think he started on the path to one of the most notable NFL insiders right off the bat. At this point in his career, though, he is one of the best in the business at breaking stories about our favorite, and least favorite, teams across the league.

Ian enrolled at Columbia University with the intention of becoming a lawyer. He majored in history and was planning on walking onto the baseball team. Little did he know that rowing and writing at the school newspaper, *the Columbia Daily Spectator*, was going to take up all his time; and once he started writing, his career in law took a backseat to his newfound love of journalism. "As soon as I started writing at *The Spectator*, I knew this was what I wanted to be. I stopped wanting to be a lawyer and started focusing on how to get into journalism." [35]

"I love telling stories. I like telling people something interesting that they've never heard before." The connection to his original idea coming into college is still alive; many lawyers need to tell stories to connect with the jury and others in the court. Ian kept that love alive while adding his love of sports to the mix. "In college, it

---

35 D.J. Podgorny, "Ian Rapoport: Relentlessly Competitive," Front Office Sports, November 7, 2016.

was cool because your face was in the daily paper and people read it, so people on campus recognized you. I liked that and getting to know some of the people I covered." There may have been a bit of ego involved as well; as with many great athletes, getting noticed isn't the number one benefit, but it doesn't hurt. [36]

Showing his worth, Ian earned a promotion to associate sports editor, which meant once a week he was required to stay at the office until 2:30 a.m. to dot the i's and cross the t's of the paper. This wouldn't have been a problem for most college kids, but Ian was on the rowing team. And if anyone knows one thing about rowing, it's that their practices are early. After staying at the office until 2:30 a.m., Ian would have to be at practice by 6:00 a.m. With a small amount of sleep in college, this ended up all being worth it because Ian was able to secure a great internship opportunity with the industry leader in sports journalism with a spot at ESPN. At ESPN, Ian worked on their ESPN Classic channel where he was able to learn about television production with the all ins and outs that come with it. [37]

After graduating from the prestigious Columbia University with an amazing internship through ESPN, Ian started to send his resume out to 311 opportunities across the country and was only able to secure two interviews. He was able to land a spot at *The Journal News* in Westchester, New York, where he spent the first two years of his journalism career. While there, he got to do what he loved most, just not at the highest level. He covered the

36   Ibid.
37   Ibid.

local high school sports teams and told stories through written words. [38]

He unfortunately—at the time—did not get offered a full-time position after two years, leading him right back to hunting for a job. Young and single, it was up to Ian to pick up his life and move wherever there was a position for him. Taking the mindset of adding to his sports writing portfolio however possible, he landed a job in Starkville, Mississippi, where he covered the Mississippi State Bulldogs football team. His time in Starkville was successful from most accounts; he got the opportunity to continue his career within a sport he loved and was able to meet his future wife while he was doing that! [39]

Ian then moved ninety miles down the road to work as a reporter, covering the Alabama Crimson Tide, an illustrious program known for their place atop college football's Mount Rushmore. During his tenure in Tuscaloosa, things started to get a little crazy. [40]

We'll hear more from Ian's story later; understanding it can help people breaking into the sports industry specifically from the journalism side of the business. Finding something you love can bring a significant amount of happiness, even if there is a little ego involved. Creating relationships will never hurt and always make sure that you're adding value as he does with all of his. Be relentlessly competitive when it comes to your profession, because if you sit back, others will have the opportunity to lap you on the track. And always be learning!

---

38 Ibid.
39 Ibid.
40 Ibid.

The more you can learn about your field, how it works, how your job works, and how your role in the company and industry work will allow you to take advantage of the information and use your relationships and competitive edge to work your way up to where you want to be.

SHARING STORIES

Ian, like myself, wanted to help share the stories of other people for the world to learn from. Doing something you love while helping others and making enough to pay your bills sounds like the jackpot to me!

Though he started in a completely different vein, he quickly realized what he wanted to do and how he wanted to do it, then worked extremely hard to make that happen. How many people can say they covered Nick Saban, Bill Belichick, and is the top NFL insider in the league? Not too many, if any at all. This is a great example of how you can continue to work hard and smart for a little amount of money, but by keeping your eyes on the prize, you will be able to get to where you need to be!

CHAPTER 6

No Such Thing as Luck

———

"Are you going to be luckier if you put yourself out there, or if you're high sitting on your mom's couch?"

DAVID MELTZER

PUT YOURSELF THERE!

Growing up, Chad Millman knew he wanted to work in sports journalism. He probably didn't know his name would become as big as it is in the sports betting space. Chad specifically wanted to work at *Sports Illustrated*(SI) since he was a young boy reading at night in his bed. "I grew up in the '80s and ESPN was a thing, but it wasn't the thing that it is now, and I hadn't had as much of an interest in television as I did in writing." Ironically, Chad would end up working for both ESPN and SI during his career in sports journalism. "The theme for me is being in the right place at the right time but also putting yourself in the right place at the right time."

Reading came easy and natural to Chad, and this allowed him to fall in love with so many stories of athletes. This also allowed him to fall in love with certain writers and how they were able to capture a story and put it on a piece of paper for others to take it. Chad reported that the books and writers who engaged him were: *Friday Night Lights*, biographies that came out about every athlete and the autobiography, George Will, Thomas Boswell, Rick Telander, and *A Season on the Brink*. By reading all these great books from authors he enjoyed, Chad was able to study how the highest-level writers crafted their stories from a young age.

Considering the times, there weren't many mediums for sports to be portrayed to an audience other than writing. "That was always my passion, and I wanted to do that. And I was in it because I wanted to be in sports, but there weren't that many outlets that were hiring people for sports back then, so I was applying everywhere I could get a job." Back in 1993, you couldn't just start a blog and get your work out there for others to check out. It was a much harder process than that. With the limited amount of mediums to use and limited number of places that would hire writers, Chad was facing an uphill battle. Even with most of the industry working against him in this manner, he was still able to fight through the adversity and continue on toward any opportunity that came his way.

After graduating college, Chad was hopeful he would land a job if he just moved to New York City. He had a small internship with *Sports Illustrated* while in school, but he had no reason to believe that that would turn into a job if he moved closer to their headquarters. But he did believe that if he moved to New York, opportunities were bound to pop up. "Certainly, I wasn't going to be considered like a leading candidate for any reason over anybody else. But I moved here, I had some money saved up, and so I felt like I've always felt like you have a better opportunity to get a job if you are where the job is."

Wanting a job at SI so badly, Chad did his best to remove any reason to *not* be hired out of the equation to ensure he gave himself the best possible chance at landing his dream job. "I just felt like I want to get in sports, I want to get in sports media, and the opportunities were going to be bigger in New York than they were anywhere else. Certainly because of SI, as I was pretty focused on that. And so, it just happened to work out like they ended up, I was interviewing all over the place, and I had gone to visit SI and three weeks after I got here, they called and said, 'We're gonna have some openings we're gonna want to hire you. We can't do it till the end of July.' So... I moved here two weeks later, got the offer, and didn't have to start for another six weeks, so I had a whole summer off."

Being closer to the position means that a potential candidate doesn't have to restructure their entire life and rebuild their foundation in a new city. Chad moved before that phone call, allowing him to tell the truth when he said he lived in New York City already to give SI the assurance this won't be a long process.

Before Chad received this phone call from SI, he was in a bit of a pickle. Living in New York City is not cheap, and needing to make money is necessary for anyone, even if you did have a couple dollars saved up as he did. When he moved, his dad handed him a bartenders' manual as a "break glass in case of emergency backup plan." "My dad handed me the book and said, 'I don't know how long this money is gonna last so you know you better start using this.' And that was that. He helped me unpack and then he was off back to Chicago."

Thankfully, Chad never had to open that manual. It got close as he was turned down for a few positions before SI gave him a call, so he never put it to use. He *did* know exactly where it was in his apartment in case he needed to go out and make some money.

Another big piece of the puzzle that Chad believed was a major reason why he was hired was simply due to familiarity. As he stated before, just because they knew him didn't mean he was going to get a job, but it surely didn't hurt. "They knew me and I was available, I really think that was it." Pretty simple; it wouldn't be hard to integrate him into the culture or teach him how to work there, but getting familiar with the staff for his internship is where the work came in.

"I had been lucky enough to spend the summer with Rick Telander, who was then, you know, on the Mount Rushmore of SI writers in the '80s. People knew who I was, because then that led to me working at SI at the Olympics in Barcelona, which is where the entire office from New York relocated for a month." That internship we spoke about before, that wasn't just any old internship. Chad was traveling abroad for school and after his program ended, he decided to travel a bit longer.

The Barcelona Olympics were coming up and with the whole SI staff relocating to cover the Games, Chad wanted to see if he could add a little something extra to his travels. "The way that my travel schedule was ending, I realized I could put myself in Barcelona and pitch myself to SI as just being an unpaid intern... So I just cold-called SI and got in touch with the guy who was running Olympic coverage he was a... senior executive there. I explained who I was and he called Rick after. I... was like this young kid just calling and pitching them, and they said yeah, it's great you work for me. And so, then they said, yeah if you're going to be in Barcelona. Come, come to the office, we'll figure out a job." Being a smart guy, Chad was able to think on his feet and realize how much opportunity could come with getting a position with SI, especially when they are covering a global mega event like the Olympics. Volunteering as an unpaid intern meant the name of the game while there was to network with the staff, and he got the perfect position for it.

"I sat behind a desk when I was like, you know, working reception in the media center at the Olympics in Barcelona, but *every single person* had to come by me. The editor of the magazine, the chief of reporters, who hired all the entry-level people, every writer had to come by and sort of, you know, say hello to me." Cold-calling SI while on a vacation to get an unpaid internship landed young Chad a position where he had the opportunity to make friends with all the people that were covering the games, and it's not like they sent just anybody over to cover the Olympics, especially in 1992. He didn't just stop at "hello" either; he looked to form relationships with all these people. "So, I got to know people I got to know what's going on. And so that was just an incredible experience." By creating real relationships with the people at SI in a time they will never forget covering the Olympic Games, Chad was able to build that familiarity that led to him landing his first full-time position with the company.

All that work Chad put in up to this point was great, but he is only at step one of his career now that he is getting paid. He now has to rise through the ranks to get to where he wants to be, and he'll need to work hard to even just keep the job he has. There are more people like Chad out there who would have done exactly what he did to get that job, so he can't let his foot off the pedal now.

The culture of SI wasn't going to be the problem. "Well, it was very hyper-competitive in *Sports Illustrated*." His first role at SI was a reporter, but all the reporters wanted to be writers. "They wanted to be Gary Smith, they wanted to be Rick Reilly, they wanted to be Rick Telander, Alex Wolff, whatever it was, Steve Rushin. That was one of the best jobs in sports, and very few people were going to get promoted from being, it was called the 'bullpen' where the reporters worked, to being writers." At this time in the early 1990s, being a writer at SI was one of the most coveted jobs in sports journalism. It was the "Murders Row" of the 1920s Yankees, it was the "Purple People Eaters" of the Minnesota Vikings '60s and '70s teams, it was the "Dream Team" from that 1992 Olympics in Barcelona Chad already worked at. These guys mastered their craft and worked harder than anyone else to make sure no one could take it from them.

WHY I DON'T BELIEVE IN LUCK, AND NEITHER SHOULD YOU!

I personally do not believe in luck; I said it earlier in the book and this is a whole chapter dedicated to it! The definition of luck is success or failure apparently brought by chance rather than through one's own actions. This makes me angry! Understanding the amount of work that goes into these high-level jobs from the previous chapters, leaving things up to "chance" does not seem like something any of these incredible sports business professionals would be interested in.

Does what Chad did sound like luck? Did he wait for something to happen, or did he go and get it? Of course, he went and got it. He did a little free work, granted at the Olympics, and was able to catapult his career even further.

KEEP GOING DOWN THE PATH

Barry Landis is one of the nicest people you will ever meet. He is the kind of person who, even if he doesn't know you, will go out of his way to help. That is always what I admired about Barry, that, and his really awesome job! Barry is a taller dude who is always relaxed and as cool as a cucumber. The more time I spent with him, the more I enjoyed his company. I met Barry at a diner I used to work at where he and his family would come in and get breakfast every weekend. It wasn't until a few years into waiting on him and his family that I asked what he did. And it wasn't until our initial interview that I found out how he got there. Barry is an Emmy Award-winning producer of NASCAR on Fox and also produces NFL on Fox, and he's been doing this for over ten years.

Barry's journey actually starts with his dad. He worked in sports television before ESPN was even a thing. "Before there was ESPN. Before there were all these cable arms, believe it or not. Public television carried the most sports, at least in this area. So, growing up in the Trenton area, my dad worked for NJPTV (New Jersey Public Television)... You had your NBC affiliate you had your ABC affiliate or CBS affiliate, then you had PBS and PBS was known for what, you know, fundraisers and, you know, art shows and things like that. But they created this niche of sports. And they did live broadcasts of almost every Rutgers basketball game, Princeton basketball and football. And eventually for my father, he would do the nightly news on NJPTV. He was a sports guy." Learning more about Barry's father and what he did is a necessity to learning about his career. It's very easy to think how his father was a major sports TV guy here in New Jersey, so Barry would put his life's work into it as well.

"It morphed into doing these live broadcasts, and then his own talk show, which he would get, you know, he had everybody from Muhammad Ali to Al Unser on his show throughout the year so that was all late '70s. And then obviously that disappeared once the ESPNs of the world took over in the '80s, so it was a nice little window." From a young age, Barry was able to see high-level sports icons speak to his dad directly in front of him. This had to have an imprint on someone's mind, especially a child's. The more he saw these athletes, shows, and live events, it eventually did become an inevitability for Barry to join the sports TV ranks. "I got a little taste of television, always liked the live events the most. You know I'd be up in the announcer booth with him. I always joke with Bill Raftery when I see him. He's become this Emmy Award-winning basketball analyst and his very first game he ever did was my dad hired and my dad was a play-by-play guy and Bill would be, he was actually still coaching and Seton Hall, I believe at the time, came on as his analyst and can't confirm this, but there's a very good possibility that in Bill Raftery's first game, his statistician and spotter was a little ten or eleven-year-old knucklehead, and it was probably me."

Getting used to being around icons and athletes from a young age made it very easy for Barry to do what he does now. He may have been a little spoiled with all those amazing people, but whoever says that is probably just a bit jealous (I'm jealous). But considering sports is an industry, it's difficult to know what you want to do within it. So many people are like you, me, and Barry, where we know if we're going to work all these hours and dedicate all this time to something, we want it to be something we love. "You kind of put off the reality of what you're going to do for a living. But in the back of my mind, I always knew that I wanted to do something that was sports-related. I contacted my dad and said, 'Hey, you know, I think I want to pursue a career behind the camera, I don't want to be in front of it.' And so, he talked to two people and I went up there (CBS). It really didn't bear any fruit, but it kind of solidified my thought that, you know, hey, this is what I want to do. This is my ticket." Barry grew up in a sports business household, so he was able to draw upon relationships that he already had (his dad) to find his way into the door. A couple lessons here to understand:

Yes, it definitely matters who you know. There are so many people trying to get these jobs that you need to know someone, you can't just be a resume in a stack of papers. The other lesson: It doesn't matter if it's your dad or not, if you're not the ideal candidate at the right time, you won't get hired. Barry understood that there was a lot at play and he could wait his time out in the sports industry before he got to doing what he really wanted.

But you never know what might come from a situation or an opportunity because, again, it's who you know! "But in that trip up to New York (CBS), a young guy who at one point interned for my dad, and I knew his sister really well, my dad helped him with an internship and public television. He was working at Major League Baseball productions. They did some of the year in highlight tapes for the, you know, individual teams and Major League Baseball really didn't oversee a whole lot of what they did was kind of an independent." By talking to the right people, meeting everyone and being nice to them, and also having his dad be a great guy, Barry was able to get a full-time job out of that trip to New York, even though it wasn't quite what he expected! He was also able to get a job close to what he wanted out of that trip too.

"That trip up to New York I told you about... for an interview at CBS, I did get to meet a few production people. And back then [at] CBS, every weekend, you'd hire local statisticians to work as production support. Well, just so happens, in 1991, the Madden Summerall crew were always at Giants Stadium. I mean, every Giant home game, they did it. If they didn't, they were in Washington. You know if they weren't Washington, they were in

Philly. So, they were all kind of close. And I would sign up and work on weekends for them as a specialty stats person." The value that Barry got from working directly with these legends of the game, the game he wanted to play, was immense. Seeing how the best in the business do something is never the easiest thing to get your hands on. But he was willing to sacrifice some of his weekend and some of his life to work with one of the most iconic broadcast teams in NFL history.

"I'm working in Major League Baseball productions, they call the Phoenix Communications the blanket for that company. I was working there, which is in Hackensack, New Jersey. Many times, I'd work the Friday night shift there, the Saturday night shift, and literally either drive or walk right up the road to Giant Stadium. Be a runner do all that kind of stuff. And the more I worked, the more calls I got from other production people. Hey, I'm doing a Rutgers basketball game or Seton Hall basketball game, the Big East Tournament. And I kept getting called to work on these different shows. And with that you get more responsibility." Many times, responsibility is either gained or taken. Barry was able to take more responsibility because he gained the trust of some very high-level people. Many of us would not sacrifice multiple years of our life for a low-level job with few rewards, but the more you do something, the better you get at it, and the more responsibility you gain, the more perks.

"I actually went to the Super Bowl in New Orleans (1989). They paid for me to go down and be one of their specialty stat guys. So, all of a sudden, things really started to cook pretty good. and I was busy seven days a week and still didn't have a pot to piss in quite honestly; but hey, it was what it was." This is also the time when Barry was very much able to focus in on what he wanted to do. Doing all different aspects of production, he was able to "test" everything out and see which direction he wanted his career to take. "So, I had a great opportunity to see post production, how to put a show together, and also live television. And it was this crash course that happened in four years that was like no other. I mean I didn't go to the beach for vacation. I didn't, you know, go to college parties and all that stuff I was pretty much locked into it. And it really solidified that live television is what I wanted to do."

When you find something you really love, sacrifices are going to need to happen. You are willing to sacrifice when you love what you do and can see how far it can take you in terms of happiness. Clearly, that was the case for Barry, and he used it to his advantage. Of course, everything is not always smooth sailing.

While at Phoenix Communications, they picked up a project, MLB International, and named Barry Producer on the project allowing him to build his resume by doing more high-level work. "In '93, they told us it was going to be our last season doing Major League Baseball International. And at that point, I got a call from the lead broadcasts associated on the Madden crew and said that I would like you to be our traveling statistician for the '93 seasons, which turned out to be CBS last season, which was a great experience. So, every weekend I traveled wherever they went, that's where I went. It was a fantastic experience. Major League Baseball international show goes belly-up.

And now CBS loses everything from the NFL. So, at the end of '93, I'm like crap. I was on such a nice little upward trajectory and all of a sudden, the bottom just fell out."

Even with everything seemingly perfect, nothing is guaranteed in the sports world! At any time, everything can come crumbling down. *But* if you did good work and have helped a lot of people, there are good things still to come. "Once Fox got the NFL, I get a phone call from a longtime CBS producer, whose name is Mike Burks, and Mike was the lead producer of the NBA on CBS. He was an NFL producer, and he asked me if I was interested in joining him at Fox as his broadcast associate. The hierarchy is you have a producer director, you have an associate director, and then you have a broadcast associate." So, while things started to look very bad, they got pretty good in only a few minutes!

"Then in '97, I took the step up to associate director, who is the person that's more in charge of commercial timings, and you sit behind the producer and director. You're a little more involved in the front benches." With more time, energy, and effort comes more responsibility!

"Then NFL Europe came around in '98 and NFL Europe, Fox got the rights to be able to broadcast that they very wisely decided they were going to send some of the younger production people who they liked, and give them an opportunity to be producers and directors. So, in the late '90s, I got the opportunity to go to Europe, you know, three months, back and forth, produce NFL Europe games, direct NFL Europe games, deal with talent, talking to them on headsets steering of broadcasts in certain directions, and literally that same year in '98, I got my first opportunity to produce an NFL game."

Barry has been producing NFL games on Fox and NASCAR events as well since 1998. As you have seen, he has done whatever it took, and even though he had great connections to the industry with his dad, it was never given to him. He was able to create his own luck by consistently putting himself in the best possible position and doing whatever was needed of him, even if it meant sacrificing his weekends and his life. Seems worth it now when you see how much he enjoys everything he does in the sports world!

IT'S BETTER TO BE GOOD THAN LUCKY

In my opinion, people believe that luck plays a very big role in those that are much higher up than them at their job, within their industry, or just in life. Too often you hear people say, "That person is so lucky to have that job," when in reality, that person worked very hard to get there. Does nepotism exist? Yes. Do some people get a bit further because who their dad is or who their mom knows? Of course. But if you truly believe that everyone that "made it" possesses rich parents or famous uncles and aunts, you put *yourself* at a disadvantage. Thinking that other people made it as far as they did because they're lucky to have well-known parents limits yourself. Understanding that many of these people worked very hard and made it on their own merit allows you to believe in yourself and kick-start your career by working harder than everyone else.

I don't believe in luck and I don't believe in coincidences. But I do believe being in the right place at the right time.

And for a very hyperbolic example, do you think you'll have a better shot getting your dream job working hard every day with focus and determination, or being high on your mom's couch? Unless the hiring agent for your dream job wants to get high with you on your mom's couch, the answer is the former. As the stories of Chad and Barry point out, there is a lot you have to go through to get to the top, but, man, it's fun up there! Being in the right place at the right time *because* they were working so hard was an instrumental way to progress and succeed in this industry!

CHAPTER 7

Keep Saying Yes

MORE YESES PLEASE!

We have already heard from Chad Millman and Ian Rapoport on how they were able to work hard enough to land some incredible jobs, but what they're doing now came from saying "yes" each chance they got!

"It wasn't so much like you had to stay uncomfortable, or you had to find ways to stay uncomfortable. You were uncomfortable because it was so competitive." The talented roster at SI made each and every one of them better because they were all competing for the same few spots. Until a new opportunity became available.

After five years at *Sports Illustrated*, Chad was presented with an opportunity to join *ESPN The Magazine*, a new offering from the worldwide leader. How did ESPN try to create something that had already been done? Go to the leader in that business and start to take the talent that was there. Many of the people on the first *ESPN The Magazine* staff came directly from Sports Illustrated. "People who are going to start up *ESPN the Magazine*, a couple of them were preeminent alumni of Sports Illustrated, including John Pasternak who was the first editor in chief of *ESPN The Magazine* and Steve Wulf who was the executive editor." Chad had many conversations over his period of time at SI with each of these people. Creating those real relationships that started all the way back when he was interning at the Olympics in Barcelona has helped him find more and more opportunities to take advantage of.

"I had sort of done enough good work at SI and stayed on the radar of Steve and his wife that when Steve went to ESPN and they were starting the magazine, I had reached out to a couple people there, and Steve kindly put in a good word for me." All opportunities are created the same though. Moving from somewhere he was familiar could have been a scary career move, but with all the people he knew at *ESPN The Magazine*, it was closer to a second home than anything else.

While his relationships helped get Chad in the door, it was really all the hard work he did along the way that the higher-ups noticed. He built up a good amount of work over his five years at SI that it made it easier for people to say yes than no when the discussions were going on. "It was a brand-new entity. I have a decent pedigree from what I had done at *Sports Illustrated* and they were looking for people who were younger and thinking differently about magazines and probably less expensive and so... I had sort of just the right amount of ability and the right background or the right sort of relationships that they're like, yeah, let's take a flyer on this guy."

While at *ESPN The Magazine*, Chad was hit with another stroke of "luck," as he calls it. A story about a bookmaker was being written by another writer and after deciding he wanted a bigger story, Chad was called upon to finish this story. This was originally going to be a quick one-page story; that eventually changed Chad's life. After the story came out, Chad reached back out to the bookmaker to see if he could write a book with him in it. "I called back the bookmaker and we spoke for a while and it was a story and he and I hit it off and it was over, like this is really interesting." With Las Vegas still being the only place in the United States where you could legally place bets, the characters that pop up in real life there are unlike any other. This led Chad down a path of creating content for this "shadow industry" that had a huge effect on sports, whether we knew it or not.

"I was sitting at my desk. I just finished talking to Joe Lupo. He was telling me about the competition that was between him and the betters and how the lines are made and how they move and I said to him, 'I gotta tell you, I feel like this is a book.'" Even though the single page story was assigned to him after another person didn't want it, Chad was able to take advantage of a situation that does not come along very often. Learning from all of the incredible people before him and staying up late at night reading as a kid prepared him for this exact moment. Seeing the story and the characters unfold before him gave him this great idea that brought his career another step further. "I started reporting it in '99, the winter of '99, it came out in March of 2001, and it completely changed the trajectory, eventually, of my career. Because ultimately, you know I got very into sports betting."

By 2008, Chad started to cover the gambling beat for ESPN and was able to dive deep into what was happening, why lines were moving, and the best picks to make. Considering this is a huge company in ESPN, owned by Disney at the time, it might not have been in their best interest to cover the illegal topic of sports betting. "Well, they didn't really want to do it. They just sort of let me keep doing it as a lark because it was interesting and I could sort of find the pockets of people who would want to do it and wanted to engage, but it wasn't gonna hurt anything." It also didn't hurt that he had a few important people in his corner that saw what the industry could possibly turn into if or when sports betting became legal across the country.

"I had a couple of advocates along the way: John Walsh, who was sort of the editorial conciliary at ESPN. He was into the idea and the way that I wanted to cover it, so he planted seeds with people. And then John Cozier... who ran ESPN digital and ultimately was my boss at the magazine, and as editorial director for ESPN digital. He was really into it; he's a very progressive guy who was always thinking about what fans are going to be interested in next and he wasn't afraid of... the political ramifications of ESPN getting into the gambling space and what that meant to relationships with the NFL and things like that."

Thinking of the fans first over the possible fallout from covering the sports betting space was a risk they were willing to take. Not only did Disney probably not love it, but their sports partners, such as the NFL, were always vehemently against the thought of gambling on their sport. So, toeing that line of giving the people what they want and not angering your parent company or partners was something they had to pay attention to at all times.

By the time the Supreme Court decided they would listen to a case about potentially making sports betting legal, or not illegal, across the country, Chad knew he put himself in a good spot. He left ESPN to join The Action Network, a company dedicated to covering the sports betting industry. The Professional and Amateur Sports Protection Act was repealed on May 14, 2018, and allowed states to allow sports gambling as they saw fit.

Chad is now the head of media for The Action Network, where he helps people understand more about the sports betting and gambling space. After working extremely hard and always going above and beyond what was expected, Chad was able to earn himself a position that he loves. Through saying yes to many opportunities and always getting himself where he needs to be, Chad has done whatever it takes.

SEE?! JUST KEPT SAYING YES!

I guess it's a combination of yes to yourself and yes to the job in front of you. Someone needed Chad to finish a story, so he said yes. But he felt that there was something extra there, too, so he kept saying yes to himself. He kept going with the sports betting opportunities, turned that story into a book, and parlayed that into more opportunities. He *asked* to start covering the beat for ESPN, and because they liked how hard he worked and how good his work was, he was able to do what he wanted!

By doing what he was attracted to, he now has an awesome job with a media company that is taking over the sports betting space, but he would have never gotten there if he didn't say yes to taking that story someone else didn't want to do!

SERIOUSLY, KEEP SAYING IT!

When we left Ian Rappaport earlier in this book, he was just starting his tenure with the University of Alabama, where things were going to start getting a bit crazy.

Current Miami Dolphins head coach (at the time) Nick Saban was in the midst of a disappointing season in terms of his insanely high standards. There were rumors of his return to the college coaching ranks, where most saw a better fit for his coaching style, and many got their wish. Immediately after the Dolphins' season ended, Saban was hired as Alabama's twenty-seventh head coach on January 3, 2007.

"When Saban got hired in 2007, my world went absolutely crazy. That's still the hardest job I've ever done, but it was cool because everybody would read it. When Nick Saban speaks, everyone wants to know what he is saying. Covering him was crazy, intense, and unbelievable." Having the opportunity to be at the forefront of the college football landscape while one of the best coaches in the history of the game made a move gave Ian a much bigger platform than expected when he took the job. It also brought Ian back to his roots of wanting people to see his name and read his stories, which happened a lot.[41]

Understanding the industry you're in and how you can take advantage of unique situations is very important within any job, but especially with positions in sports.

41 D.J. Podgorny, "Ian Rapoport: Relentlessly Competitive," Front Office Sports, November 7, 2016.

When Ian saw a position open up for the *Boston Herald* after three years of covering Alabama, he took his shot. The position was to cover the New England Patriots halfway through their unprecedented dynasty that lasted over twenty years. Even though the job asked for NFL experience, Ian was able to leverage his time within the media circus that was Alabama football and Nick Saban.

"I've gotten a lot of jobs that I didn't think I was qualified for. There was a lot of luck involved and I was fortunate to have a bunch of editors that were willing to take a real chance on someone who didn't deserve it." Good people make good things happen, and while Ian may not think he was qualified for certain roles, he was able to get them through hard work and framing his experiences in a way that allowed others to take that chance on him. Ian may call this luck, but I would say it was really the willingness to work and say yes.[42]

For another three years, Ian was following around a coach and a team that were always making history. While at the Super Bowl, when the Patriots faced off against the New York Football Giants (no, not that one, the second one), Ian was approached by the NFL Network about a potential opportunity they thought he would be suited for. Finally, Ian did not need to shower the country with his resume; he was the one being courted now, but he didn't even know it.

"I sat down in the conference room, not even dressed for an interview, wearing jeans and a sweater. I sat down for an hour while they fired questions at me about the Patriots, journalism, reporting, my background, what I

---

42   Ibid.

would do in certain situations, just question after question." After this hour of being grilled by top brass at the NFL, Ian was still confused on what exactly they had brought him there for. "The NFL Network interviews a lot of people at the Super Bowl." This could have just been a formality, or a weird way of just getting to know someone. They eventually told him that they were looking for a new TV reporter and they were interested in him. From his short internship at ESPN, Ian has been familiar with the television side of things, even if his skills were rusty. Even with this against him, he was confident he was about to receive a new position at the NFL.[43]

"I remember leaving there and calling my wife, explaining to her that we might get a new job. I told her, 'I know this is crazy and that they interview a lot of people, but I'm telling you something just happened and I think we may have to move.'" This was a move to Dallas, where after a year of crushing his work, he was promoted to NFL insider. This is the position most of us know Ian for today, the man with all the information that is coming out of the league.[44]

With all the moving and shaking necessary to make it in the journalism field, Ian has figured out his secret sauce for his quick advancement into a job he loves. One part relentless competitiveness, one part unquenchable thirst for learning, one part relationship-building. The combination of these three traits creates a clear correlation on how Ian was able to rise so quickly from starting his writing career in college to becoming one of the most well-known figures in NFL media.

---

43 Ibid.
44 Ibid.

Sports are competitive, and one thing I have found out through the process of interviewing for and writing this book is that the people in the media and business of sports are also just as competitive as Ian. "I hate losing. I hate getting beat. I hate watching other people have stories that I didn't have or be behind the news. I hate it. I like when I break a story, especially a really big one; that's an awesome feeling. I hate losing way, way more." [45]

"There is a lot of studying my competitors to find out how to operate and developing how I would do it. I tend to do my job differently from a lot of people, but it's really important to sit back and really figure things out, as opposed to jumping in and thinking you know what you're doing. I have taken a lot of jobs where I didn't know what I was doing at all, so I've had to analyze how others have done it, how I would ideally do it, and put all of that together to come up with a methodology." [46]

Learning what needs to be done within each of his roles may have taken Ian "about a year to have any idea what [he's] doing," but it allowed him to learn how to do everything correctly while having his feet to the fire. Watching some of the greatest football coaches of all time in Nick Saban and Bill Belichick and their process-oriented structure probably didn't hurt. [47]

Ian's research has led to some specific processes that continue to help him succeed. "Figure out who to talk to. Spend some time, say, 'Who is going to know this information?'... Identifying sources is one of the most valuable

---

45   Ibid.

46   Ibid.

47   Ibid

things and, a lot of times, it's in places you wouldn't imagine. No source is too small. You never know who can help you or who you can help." [48] Of course, as most of these stories do, it comes back to adding value to others and building relationships with the ones around you. You may be able to help them, they may be able to help you, and there is a certainty that everybody knows somebody!

Understanding Chad's and Ian's stories can help people breaking into the sports industry a few different ways, as with all of these stories, but specifically from the journalism side of the business. Finding something you love can bring a significant amount of happiness, even if there is a little ego involved. Creating relationships will never hurt, and always make sure that you're adding value, as they do with all of their relationships. Be relentlessly competitive when it comes to your profession because if you sit back, others will have the opportunity to lap you on the track. And always be learning! The more you can learn about your field, how it works, how your job works, and how your role in the company and industry works, it will allow you to take advantage of the information and use your relationships and competitive edge to work your way up to where you want to be.

HOW MANY YESES?

How many times do you have to say yes for this all to be worth it? Unfortunately, there is no set number. For everyone it will be different, but you'll know it when you see it! The more yeses lead to more opportunities to say yes, which lead to more opportunities to show your stuff.

---

48 Ibid

Will it all work out? Of course not. But you won't know which one will be the most important until many moons later. Saying yes to what you think is your dream job or a great client may seem obvious in the beginning because all of the things that can go right! This also might be something that teaches you that a dream job isn't much of a dream, or that client isn't who you're going to be looking for moving forward.

In my business, I got an amazing client that paid well and I was able to help significantly over the span of about eight months. Over the time I was working there, I was noticing more and more things that I didn't love, not about the client, but about the system. I stayed because the money was great and I was still accomplishing my goal of helping the athletes I wanted to help. The relationship eventually ended and I realized I did not want a client like that ever again! It was a bittersweet ending, but I'm very glad I said yes to the situation and that it pushed me down the road closer to what I'm meant to do.

And let's clarify this for the people in the back; you can't possibly say yes to everything. You have to pick your spots. If you have the time and desire, and want to learn the skills and knowledge of a position, then say yes. If there is an incredible networking opportunity, you should say yes, but if there isn't much for you to gain, or it will eat up too much of your time, don't feel bad about saying no at all!

CHAPTER 8

Forks in the Road

———

"When you come to a fork in the road, take it!"

YOGI BERRA

START SOMEWHERE ELSE?

Just because you aren't in the sports industry now, doesn't mean you can't get there. Sometimes not starting in the sports industry is the best thing you could do. A big piece of this book has been to show you how there are many different jobs in the sports industry, because it's just that, an industry. There are accountants and marketers and salespeople and operations experts just like every other industry. In this chapter, I'm excited to highlight some of my friends who have started outside the sports industry but have used their skills, knowledge, and desire to become experts at something outside of the industry, and used them to get in.

Finding ways into the industry through the "back" or "side" doors has been very useful for some people. This can be used so you can become an expert at something like marketing, sales, or partnerships and take that info to crush it for sports. This is also another way to differentiate yourself, sometimes for the better, sometimes for the worse. Taking this route can also give you more leeway when you look at your bank account; it's been highlighted throughout that those first few years won't pay the best, but the experiences are invaluable. You can get a similar value with some more money going a different route.

FROM NASA TO SPORTS VENTURE CAPITAL

Jessica David is currently the marketing manager at Intel Sports and the former director of marketing at sports centric venture capital firm SeventySix Capital. SeventySix Capital "invests at the epicenter of sports and tech," which is a rebrand that they took on only a few years ago, right as they were bringing Jess onto the team. While I could not find the exact size of SeventySix Capital's funds, the venture capital market as a whole had over 130 billion dollars invested into it during the 2019 calendar year. [49]

Jess grew up on the bustling East Coast, from New York City to the Greater Philadelphia area, which as you will see is a huge contributing factor to her ability to get things done. On the outside, she's small and always smiling; on the inside, she has a strong will to do what she has to to get the job done, even before she has it. Jess might not appear to have a quintessential NYC attitude, but she does show that there is a side of her that will strongly take a stand to do the right thing. She decided

49 Cassie Ann Hodges, "US Venture Capital Investment Surpasses $130 Billion in 2019 for Second Consecutive Year," NVCA, January 14, 2020.

to leave the chilly north for a southern college experience when she decided to take her talents to James Madison University in Harrisonburg, Virginia. Harrisonburg is a small city just below fifty thousand people, compared to the 8.6 million in New York City.

She attended the school in the small mountain town on a business scholarship but ended up majoring in graphic design, her true love. The love is real and she utilized her skills in the freelance space where she won a contest for the ability to work for NASA on a specific project. Yes, *that* NASA, the National Aeronautics and Space Administration. She spent several years working for Chester County, another governmental agency, this time on a full-time basis where she learned the meaning of "process." She looked for a more fast-paced opportunity and was able to find a job with Meyer, an architectural design firm just outside of Philadelphia.

When Jess was getting to the end of her college career, she was already starting her preparation into the work-force. "When I first graduated from college, I applied to, I think, seventy-five jobs, and just took every interview I got." Understanding was always a goal of hers, whether that was the job market or the specific jobs themselves. Preparation has always been one of Jess' strong suits, and she's been practicing this skill since college. "It was good to have practice and it was useful to ask meaningful questions and see what types of responses I would get to really see if I could, you know, come at the situation from all angles and see where the differences lie within organizations. Those are fun conversations to me." Doing the work and knowing what's coming and where the opportunities are coming from has allowed Jess to have the leverage in whatever situation she is in.

Jess spent her first few years at the Chester County Intermediate Unit within the Pennsylvania Department of Education. If you know how work happens in government, you would agree that it all takes a very long time to get things done. Checks, balances, and getting approval from every person necessary while great in certain situations, it can be tough for individuals that like to move fast. After learning how to do things "the right way," Jess found a position at an architectural design firm where she was the new kid pitching ideas on how to help this twenty-five-year-old company create brand new revenue streams.

"I was their first graphic designer, went to the marketing department, and they wanted somebody who could build something, so we did just that. We built a new global branding studio within the firm that was available for hire for existing clients, including graphic design, wayfinding, marketing materials, and more. It was an exciting way to grow the business while building a team." While the idea was all well and good, it was much easier said than done. The necessity to go to each project manager specifically to pitch the project to them may have been a difficult task, but it gave her the ability to understand the specific needs of each person and how to craft her ideas around what they were looking for. Sitting across the table from one person and understanding how their end of the business worked helped Jess again with her preparedness when pitching, but also how she crafted a message, which she does a lot now! Despite her status relative to management at the time, Jess overcame each objection by preparing for what the questions would be before they were asked.

Several years later, Jess saw that there was a director of marketing job available at SeventySix Capital but did not think she was qualified for the position. Her parents and husband got together and convinced her to give it a shot and apply. She reached out to a former alumnus of hers and he gave her the information. "When this job posting came up, I considered myself to be unqualified. I made a million reasons why I wasn't good enough for a director position at a venture capital firm. It just seemed like this crazy goal that I would never be able to reach, even though I had worked with this team before. I really needed to prove myself to stand out as a candidate," Jess recalled. When she was working over at Meyer, SeventySix Capital was a client that she helped create for; this gave her personal knowledge of their business and the people within it. Even someone as supremely talented with all the experience, ingenuity, and intelligence you'd want from an employee still did not fully believe in her potential. Thankfully, her family was there to support her and push her to give it a shot. "It was really one night at dinner, my husband and my parents just, I think they were in cahoots and they totally just bombarded me and were like, 'You have this, you can do this, go call Chad right now.'" Jess made that phone call to her soon-to-be colleague Chad Stender, who was more than delighted to point her in the direction of the job posting and gave her some insight on the position.

After her conversation with Chad, she was ready to take the leap of faith and throw her name in the hat for the job opening. Jess found out what the requirements of the job were and decided to take matters into her own hands—to show what she could do, rather than just say it. She went to an event that the managing partner of the business was speaking at to showcase her skills. "He was speaking at an event in my town and I just showed up as if I already had the job to prove that I could do it. Part of the job description included doing social media so I said, 'Okay, I'm going to go to this event, and I'm going to pretend that I'm doing his Twitter, his Facebook, his LinkedIn.' I took all these photos and videos and put together a report with social copy and strategy afterwards and said, 'Here's what your day would have looked like if I was logged into your accounts.'" She acted as if she already had the job and did above and beyond what was expected for the job, let alone the interview. This coupled with the incredible work she had already done for SeventySix Capital when they were her client clearly separated Jess from the rest of the candidates.

Jess was obviously offered the job at SeventySix Capital and became the director of marketing of the sports-focused venture capital firm. "Director of marketing" goes much further than just marketing for SeventySix Capital; as any job in a sports-based or smaller-sized company, Jess had a lot to do. "We are excited to have Jessica join our team," stated Chad Stender [50], Director of Operations at SeventySix Capital. "Her background in graphic design, photography, web design, and marketing will help

50 "SeventySix Capital names Jessica Romanelli Director of Digital Marketing," SeventySix Capital, April 27, 2017.

enhance SeventySix Capital's brand, boost our strategic marketing efforts with entrepreneurs and investors, and she will work with our portfolio companies too." Jess' preparedness is something we all can learn from. From the almost seventy-five applications she submitted when leaving college, to needing to pitch multiple business units within her own company, to completing the tasks of a job she did not yet have, she used this attribute to land a job. Jess has since moved on from SeventySix Capital to work for Intel as a marketing manager for their sports partnerships.

UNDERSTANDING YOUR STRENGTHS

Jess understood what she was good at and what she wanted to do. She knew that by taking advantage of the relationships she had, she could get much further (with some help from her family). But knowing that her marketing background could be utilized in another fashion, she ran with it!

She learned along the way at all of her stops and was able to take pieces from each job she had outside of the sports world and apply them to an industry she was much more passionate about.

INTERNET TITANS IN SPORTS

If you've been on the Internet in the late 2010s and early 2020s, the name Vaynerchuk has probably come across your timeline, news feed, or a friend said it aloud. The reason being Gary Vaynerchuk, more commonly known as Gary Vee, is all over the place inspiring others to be the best version of themselves in a way that connects with millennials and Gen Zers. He's a favorite of mine from the way he looks at how the world works and why people do what they do.

His younger brother has followed in his footsteps to some extent, a little less rah-rah and a lot less profanity, but he is an extremely hard worker that will do what is necessary to get things done. AJ worked with Gary at VaynerMedia, a preeminent digital marketing agency that understands the Internet much more than most companies do. There, Gary as the CEO and AJ as the COO, they help a significant number of brands amplify their message to their target audience by understanding how the Internet works, acts, and reacts.

In 2016, AJ decided to leave VaynerMedia, a company he helped create, for a few reasons. One big reason was his Crohn's. He was diagnosed at nineteen and his life changed in an instant. "When I was diagnosed at nineteen, it flipped my world upside down. Wrapping your head around the fact that you have an incurable disease is really something. It hit me hard at first, but over time I was able to gain perspective and I'm beyond grateful for the life that I live. I want to emphasize that I am okay." Thankfully for AJ and his family, his case is not as severe and manageable. But it still takes away from running at full throttle at all times. "That being said, I came to the conclusion that I no longer could or wanted to maintain my current lifestyle. My Crohn's case isn't severe, but it does have a daily impact on my life and has led to numerous trips to the emergency room and even a stomach surgery a few years back."

With this decision in mind, AJ decided to take about twelve months off from working to spend time with his family, to enjoy the time away, and to form the career he wanted. "A big reason I wanted to leave was that I wanted to, I aspire to identify a career that I was in more control of and that had more flexibility to accommodate some of the health issues that I face in regards to my Crohn's disease." The understanding was that if he could spend less time at work and more time taking care of himself, he would feel better on a daily basis. And while he wanted to make sure he was in control of his career, he also wanted to make sure that the business he created was going to be put in the best possible situation to succeed. "It was primarily driven by my own desire for what I wanted my career to look like. A big aspect of me leaving was, I felt that if I didn't leave then I may never leave. And it wasn't that I was unhappy. And a not often told aspect of the story is that I gave Gary, you know, as far as notice goes, more than twelve months' notice, so we actually came together and said, 'Hey, I need to leave, but I'm not going to leave tomorrow, I'm not gonna leave in thirty days or whatever, like, I'm gonna leave when it's okay for me to leave.' So it took over a year for us to hire my replacement and set up the infrastructure to feel comfortable that the time was right." Understanding that he was going to leave but having the respect for his brother and the company that he built shows that AJ is much more about the people that surround him than himself.

Those twelve months quickly became much less with AJ only taking four months off to spend away from work. He was excited to get back to work on something that he could get up and get excited for everyday. "I... wanted to blend business and sports as much as possible cuz they're my two biggest passions." Combining these passions allowed AJ to have ideas to reimagine the athlete representation business and leave his absence early. "I also felt that the athlete representation industry needed a shake-up. It needed some injection of fresh blood, and a unique perspective, that was another aspect that made it enticing."

With his background in media, marketing, and the digital space, AJ saw a better way for athletes to make money and create a legacy for themselves to allow their families to live better. The average length of an NFL player is 3.3 years; helping to extend the life of the career off the field is something that will impact lives for many potential generations. When you consider most NFL athletes get drafted at twenty-one years old, many of them are out of the league before their twenty-fifth birthday. Finding more ways to help these athletes create more long-term wealth is how VaynerSports is succeeding. "The football aspect is first and foremost, and obviously the contract is the Lion's share of the income that a player will most likely receive, but we felt that the industry as a whole almost was complacent with what their role was, and I feel like athletes hold the ball as individuals. A large reason for that is things like social media exposing them to things that are more important and more advantageous for their career. I think there were athletes that really set the trend of business and entrepreneurship and investing being the cool thing to do as an athlete, which is huge." Knowing the contract is important, AJ quickly realized that the negotiations he was doing for his VaynerMedia clients was on a completely other level than an NFL player's deal. "I think transparently the contract aspect is interesting; negotiating with an NFL team is not difficult. The best way I compare is that I had clients at VaynerMedia that I negotiated against. And with that, all thirty-two NFL teams combined times two were not of the size market cap and of the magnitude of that client." He knew above all he'd be able to impact the athletes on another level and was not worried about the contract negotiations in the least.

For that reason, AJ knew he could change the game. "It's a network thing, right, where we are getting introduced to players through existing people in our ecosystem who have an attachment or a tie to that player. So that was a big one, right, look at some of our best, strongest, and earliest clients. It was a referral basis of somebody that we knew in the world of business; it was in our ecosystem, in our sphere, and we're able to make a warm intro." By being in the business and media spaces, athletes were always around the Vaynerchuk brothers. Through these natural connections, they were able to find athletes to help and pair them with the companies that could utilize their services, always thinking how they can help all parties involved.

He does admit that Gary's gigantic following does help. "Then another big piece is that Gary has a large following, and we actually have had players. We've had numerous sit-downs with players who literally just DM my brother and say, 'Hey, I want to learn more about VaynerSports, I'm thinking about leaving my agent can we talk.'" Since VaynerSports is still a young company, they do their best to lean into what they are known for in the spaces that they are known in. "It's a reputation business, right, it's a service-based business and a lot of it's on the reputation and capabilities of individuals. And so, if you've been following my brother's content for years and you really believe in his message. It's an easy leap to make to assume that his athlete representation firm will follow those guidelines."

Coming at it from a long-term perspective and understanding that there is so much to legacy and these athletes' careers, AJ and VaynerSports are making a name for themselves on the marketing end of athlete representation. "One of our clients is vegan, and we were able to get him an endorsement deal with a publicly traded vegan-based company in which he was able to get equity before their IPO. And so, that's just a great example where I think a lot of agents and agencies were taking the cash that was offered initially, but our background and [our client's] willingness to be a little bit riskier and go for the larger upside allowed him to have a much better return than the simple transaction of cash."

Through these types of equity deals and understanding the industry and market while having a wealth of knowledge in the media world, VaynerSports has been set up to crush the athlete representation game. Coming from a completely different industry has its perks when you can apply the skills, knowledge, and desire formerly focused on the previous spot with a new goal. AJ is also able to leverage his brother's brand and all the relationships he was able to build over the years as the COO of a huge marketing and media company to a now granular outcome.

CHANGING THE GAME

AJ has been able to find a way to help people and change a longstanding game that has been lagging behind. When you move in a fast-paced world like media and marketing with his now famous brother, he's been able to see what happens when you do really good work in an efficient way. He was able to see there was a space in an industry that he loved and could use those same attributes to improve upon it. This allowed him and his team to grow VaynerSports quickly and show value to athletes in a different way than they have seen before. Disrupting the space with a huge name behind it has allowed AJ to put everything he learned, experienced, and became good at to use in a way that brings more joy to him and more value to the industry!

CHAPTER 9

Blaze Your Own Trail

"Content is King, context is God."

GARY VEE

SPORTS BUSINESS MEDIA

Adam White is the founder and current CEO of Front Office Sports (FOS) and recent recipient of the prestigious Forbes 30 Under 30 honor. He started the company as a place to house his work and ensure he would have a job offer once his time was finished at the University of Miami.

Adam did not want to deal with the interview process after college; he knew sports was a "know somebody" kind of industry. "What do I do to make sure at least I have some sort of connections by the time I graduate so I can go and work and I don't have to worry about going to the job application process?" He decided it would be more productive if he created an outlet to allow him to speak with industry veterans and place those conversations online for people to learn from. By creating the news site, it was an easy execution for him to discuss topics with people that he normally wouldn't be able to speak with. "Well, if I'm going to do informational interviews for class projects, I'm going to do informational interviews and publish them to meet people in the space."

The original theme of Front Office Sports was to share the stories of the people working in the sports business arena rather than reporting news within it. Taking this approach has helped Adam get better at the interview process—now speaking with well-known figures in the media space like Erika Nardini of Barstool Sports, Howard Mittman formerly of Bleacher Report, and Gary Vaynerchuk of VaynerMedia—but also start to make connections in a space where networking and knowing how to help others is key. This is also another instance of someone understanding that if you want to get paid to do something, particularly in the sports industry, you have to do it for free first.

With some small success in the beginning, Adam was able to get some friends and schoolmates from The U (the University of Miami) to get on board with his project. Up until about eighteen months ago as of this interview, Adam was still pouring mimosas to thirsty college kids before the big game at a bar down by his school. The success may seem like it came quickly, but in reality, the FOS team has been grinding to make this dream become a reality. "I just got to the point where it's like, we just started making enough money to where I could pay my bills." In reality, isn't that all we need at a young age? "Do what you have to do to get by and find a way to make it work" was essentially Adam's mantra for the first few years after college. We all have twenty-four hours in a day; if it takes working an extra job as a bartender to make your dream come true, you have to do it. By no means was this a glamorous lifestyle, but it worked.

The ability to put his work somewhere and connect with others is great, but once this project turned into a business, everything had changed. There were multiple roadblocks that he and his team faced along the way to becoming a legitimate business. He first needed to learn how to amplify his stories and the best ways to publish through his site and through social media so more people could see his work. That is all well and good, but if no one knew who you were, why would they look at your content? "The biggest roadblock we faced early on was that no one knew who we were, so trying to build legitimacy and brand awareness took a concerted effort to produce high-quality content and rely on the people we were interviewing to help us spread the message of the publication." After all, why would people pay attention to a nobody? So building awareness and legitimacy through having the subjects share their content was a huge portion of why they are successful today. And now with multiple full-time staffers, they need to find a way to make money in an industry that is getting harder and harder to make money in. The number one rule of business is to stay in business, and they have been able to do that so far; but the monetization of their publication has to be done properly to ensure the long-term growth of the publication.

To work past these roadblocks, Adam and the FOS team did whatever needed to be done. Specifically, his team has stepped up, including his number two, Russ Wilde Jr.

"I think that's what makes us work, right. It's like, I don't think either of us are too caught up or worried about what it is when it comes down to, like, who does what, what does who and, like, you know, it's just all about, like, how do you move the needle. And I think there's not been a lot of ego between both of us in terms of, like, you know, some days I'm, I can admit he knows better than I do, and other days I know things better than he does, and we play off each other." Building a successful business with your head down will ensure the need for a great team around you to help facilitate and delegate, and to make sure nothing falls through the cracks. It's also great when your team can laugh with you as well. A running joke between Adam and Russ always brings them back to center to help them realize that what they do is important, but it's not life or death. "If only we sold chicken sandwiches," has been something they say to each other on what probably has become a daily basis. When I asked Adam he said, "What could be easier than selling chicken sandwiches?"

Front Office Sports is five years into its ten-year over-night success journey, and as we have established, Adam has been at the helm driving the bus. He understands what is expected of him at this point and is willing to do whatever needs to be done to continue down this path. FOS has a specific brand, clean and minimal when it comes to the site with great in-depth reporting on the content side. They even have utilized the animation and design studio Tykes to give all of their employees a unified image that helps solidify their brand and take a few years off their age.

This started as a way for him to publish his interviews with successful sports business media members, but there isn't as much publishing he does now with having to run the business. Adam is currently the host of *Office Hours*, the Front Office Sports podcast, but outside of that, much of his time is continuing to keep the company growing and keeping the brand where it needs to be so it can be around whether he is there or not. "It's like an NBA in a box, and it's everything that you've ever asked for so you do this and you spend three, four, or five years building a team, building brands, laying the groundwork for a sustainable business that you know that the next step is now. It's like, how do we get to the point where, theoretically, and God forbid this ever happened, Russ and I could freaking get hit by bus and we could no longer be here but FOS would still live on and that's where you have to get to."

Adam has been ready for this task since he put his life into building this company. Now with fourteen full-time employees, Adam is partially responsible for their success, whether that's the resources they need for themselves or the security of having a job. "These people can go home and pay for their kids' college tuition and pay for their kids' shoes or pay for their apartment or whatever, go out with their friends, take vacations, right, so I don't know, that's more about why it's so much fun, because every day you wake up and it's fun and stressful every day you wake up, but you have, you know, thirteen people whose theoretical livelihood is counted on." Adam is willing to take this journey head-on, head-down, wherever it leads him. Are you willing to do whatever it takes to continue to push forward and run through a brick wall?

IF YOU BELIEVE, YOU WILL RECEIVE

Believing in yourself is one of the more important things you can do in any aspect of your life. Through understanding your own strengths and weaknesses, you can understand what you can, should, and shouldn't do. On top of that, you also need to understand the space you want to enter.

Adam had some work done and thought of a great way to get that information out there while making sure that he could promote others and himself. Things started to change a bit and he realized that it could become much more than that!

Adam was able to see that there was really only one person covering the sports business world from a media company standpoint. Knowing some other companies in the space were doing things a bit differently, he wanted to get on that train and cover from a standpoint of breaking news.

Believing in his idea and thinking that it could become something big was the best thing he could have ever done. Front Office Sports is growing hand over fist, bringing great content to the sports world.

CREATING CONTENT

Jack Settleman is a content creator who has been able to amass a huge following by staying consistent, staying on brand, and having fun with what he does! Jack started his content journey on Snapchat, where he has millions and millions of views and he's spread that audience to a podcast, a YouTube page, and other social platforms. Jack is a soft-spoken dude that has dirty blonde hair and can be found more times than not yelling into a camera about Lamar Jackson and his Baltimore Ravens.

Knowing he always wanted to be in the sports industry, Jack realized that whatever needed to be done, needed to be done. "I knew I wanted to actually work in sports. I think a lot of people want to consume sports on the weekends and nights but go to a different job because, I mean, the sports industry is very tough, it doesn't pay the greatest when you're just getting started. So, I always want to be in the business of sports, I started by stringing lacrosse sticks. I was from Maryland, so we'd restring many [lacrosse] sticks and sell them—you know to classmates, stuff like that. So I just always knew I wanted to be on the business side as well." Like many people in this book, Jack was willing to do whatever it took to make money in the sports industry. "I really didn't have a clue, even in my senior year. I was like, I don't even know what marketing sports really means, like, I get the idea of it but then, like, a KPI, what's a KPI? They don't teach you all that in school, they teach you random stuff." Jack is a graduate of the University of Texas, and a great education can only get you so far in business and in life. Actually doing the work is what's going to get you that experience that you need.

Jack thinks Texas is back, by the way.

While at Texas, Jack wanted to start making money. That's when the ideas started rolling! "So, my sophomore year of college with my roommate we had some time… And I was like, let's sell phone cases, like we'll get designs, we'll kind of use players, you know, we did that gray line of likeness and stuff like that. So, there were those, then we went to print on demand. Well, we did really fun stuff and that was that. We worked with John Wall and Mohamed Sanu, some fun guys, but we were marketing all through social media: so everything was Twitter, Instagram, and buying ads. Which led me to just fall in love with social media and be like, this is an awesome platform. Okay, I'm tired of paying these accounts, big money. I just want to have my own." Jack decided that getting into the game and seeing where and why his money was being spent to make more money was the best option.

Being a smart guy, Jack realized he could start to create his own content and get other people and businesses, like his, to pay him money while also promoting his own stuff! "The first game I ever shot content for was Texas vs. Oklahoma and Baker Mayfield. We lost that game, but it was a fun game. So that's kind of where it's been over two years ago, how I got into Snap and Instagram. There's like so many people on Instagram; Twitter was pretty much dying in the sense of being able to build; Snap was just so young. I then just fell into the wormhole that is social media."

Everybody has a Snapchat, and everybody has an Instagram account. So how do you go about building that following? "There's a side of the Internet and social media that even those people aren't aware of, and that are these fourteen to nineteen-year-old kids running the world through Kik Messenger and through WhatsApp, and they are trading shout-outs, they're doing paid shout-outs, they're driving app installs, downloads, etc." The

Internet is a crazy place... "They have billions of views, tons of followers, they have these massive networks. So you know, one thousand bucks, and they shout me out and I'm posting good content every day, while I'm awake, every thirty minutes. So you can imagine thousands of pieces of content a day, and that just kind of builds and then it snowballs into, okay, now you have a big enough base to where people are going to share with their friends to kind of grow, and then I reinvest. I'd make money from brands. I just do that again."

Investing in yourself is the best thing you can do across all of life. In terms of social media, it works just as well. Finding the underground parts of the Internet where other creators exist will help you spread your brand as long as you're willing to pay for it. You are also going to need to stay consistent with what you're doing on these platforms. No one will follow you if you're posting occasionally and it's not even that great!

By creating and earning a following, Jack has been able to land some amazing positions for full-time positions. He's worked at the Action Network, a sports betting media company, and has landed a role as a content manager at Whistle Sports, a sports content start-up company. Through these positions, Jack is able to use his influence in the social media space to drive traffic and try new things out to help his companies succeed!

FANTASY SPORTS AS A PROFIT CENTER

Jason has become a very good friend of mine. Throughout this book, you've seen that I've been able to enjoy one of my favorite things, which is talking into a microphone on the radio. This is all because of Jason. He is a medium height, thicker man that has a great beard and a slick haircut. Jason has been into fantasy sports for a while and sports betting, but only since it's been legalized, of course. Jason's story is an interesting one and I'm excited I get to tell it in this book!

Jason has always worked very hard and done very well for himself. He has a consulting business and has worked with some impressive companies where he helps them figure out their vision and apply it. He keeps doing his thing but along the way realized there might be a little more to what he wants to do. "It all started when my wife had this crazy idea to write a book. So, we kind of started that. And I kind of shrugged it off like, 'Why the hell would I write a book? I don't like writing.' And then I read a lot of books so it kind of made sense to me to write a book, something that not many people do, so let me just think about this, but then I kind of brushed it off. Then some guy messages me and says, 'Hey, you ever thought about writing a book about your consulting business?' Me being naive, I said, 'If I ever wrote a book I'd write about my daily fantasy sports career and not consulting, that's a lot more exciting, talking about going to the Playboy Mansion rather than consulting for other businesses.' But I took it as a sign, If my wife is telling me, and now an Instagram bot is trying to sell me on writing a book, I probably should write a book."

Listen to the universe! There is no such thing as coincidences, there is no such thing as luck. And the only way these things don't exist is if you believe they don't! Once you believe they don't, things start to happen. If your wife tells you to do something and you don't do it, but a few weeks later a computer algorithm tells you to do the same thing, you should probably do that. These things aren't mistakes or glitches in the Matrix; it's the universe telling you to do something, but only if you believe that it is, otherwise, just keep scrolling on your iPhone. "The sign that officially made it happen was my wife, and then it was the universe kind of telling me, 'Hey, do this,' and I did it, and then basically had no intention to make a website." But we all know this story; we wouldn't be in here if he left it for dead there.

"I started talking to my friends; they said, 'Listen, how are you going to promote this book?' I'm like, 'I was gonna put it out there and see what happens.' They're like, 'No you can't do that.' Then like three or four weeks in I'm like, 'Alright, so I guess I got to start podcasting and I have to start a website,' so I literally recruited a developer and a couple people to help out and start this website, and with no serious plans. And then, you know, my entrepreneur self kicked in, and then it was full throttle from there. So the idea is like, alright, I guess I gotta do this now because I can't just release the book and then the brand kind of dies with the book. If you don't have a lot of money or your publisher behind you, it's not going to get so far."

Creating something for fun because the universe told you to do something can lead to so many amazing places. It's also something that will be able to help people along the way. Jason isn't just writing this book because he likes fantasy sports; he's writing the book because he's won over five hundred thousand dollars playing fantasy sports. His knowledge is second to none and he has the opportunity and ability to help a lot of people make a lot of money. Through this, *Win Daily* was born.

After building out a website and a place for people to learn, Jason started to build out a community and got his friends to join him on this journey by becoming writers. Through the lens of helping other people make money, Jason and his team were able to hit the ground running and he saw an opportunity in the market for a company like his. "There's so many sites out there now that people are playing on. They're going in blind. They're risking a bunch of money, they're losing a bunch of money, and they're playing daily fantasy sports, you build a lineup and you go against other people doing the same thing. And this industry has evolved in the last seven or eight years out there, and there is a lot of sharp money and there are people playing this professionally and they're trying to take your money. They're trying to take my money and they're trying to win all the money, and it's serious business. And there's people winning. Like, turned this into business, they only do this and they're making a million dollars a year." With the amount of money that is flowing throughout this industry, the opportunity to create your own business that can be a resource in the industry is huge. The fantasy football industry encompasses over seven billion dollars on median estimates, and over ten billion dollars on the high end. This gives many people like Jason the chance to start a business, help some people, and make some money.

Since sports betting has been legalized, the fantasy sports and sports betting markets have started to merge.

This has allowed *Win Daily* to bring on more seasoned veterans of handicapping and sports betting games to help their community members win even more money. The size of the sports betting market is currently significantly bigger than the fantasy sports market, even though it's only been legalized outside of Las Vegas for two years. There has been over twenty-seven billion dollars in *legal* wagers since May of 2018, with the illegal market still being much bigger.[51] With more states legalizing sports betting every day, Jason and the *Win Daily* team are taking the same mentality they had for fantasy sports and putting it into sports betting.

HELPING OTHERS

If you can find something that other people love just as much as you do and you can help them make money with it, there is a business to be founded. Jason saw this opportunity to bring people together and help them make money through fantasy sports, something a lot of people enjoy, and he's been able to create relationships and help others, and everybody has come out positive from it.

SEE IT, TAKE IT

When you think of HBO Sports, you think of boxing. Their coverage has been synonymous with the sport for a long time now, and it's looked at as the pinnacle of coverage on a single sport. In recent months as of writing this book, HBO has dropped its boxing coverage and is now shifting. But how did it get to the point of being one of the most respected media entities in the business?

---

51 Legal Sports Report, "US Sports Betting Revenue and Handle," Last Updated: October 12, 2020.

That's where our friend Mark Taffet comes in. Mark is a very nice gentleman with a great smile and slicked back hair. He normally wears glasses and, when needed, a very nice suit. Mark has been in the boxing game for over twenty years and has even moved on to helping athletes with their management and marketing needs. How Mark got into the game, or created the game, is the better story.

Mark was always smart growing up and graduated from Rutgers University, The State University of New Jersey. He then took his talents to The Wharton School of Business at the University of Pennsylvania where he got his MBA. After school was finished, Mark's credentials were good enough that he had eighteen job offers to choose from. He took a spot at General Foods in their Birds Eye Frozen Food division. "I worked in the new business development group. I was a finance member who did all the financial models and analysis, and I worked with a marketing person and an operations person meeting a guy in Iowa who worked in the fields who grew the corn, and our job was to put together new products, introduce them into the marketplace for six months, and then turn them over to the established brand. And I did that for about a year and a half. And I got very antsy because I saw that they had a graduating class mentality. People got promoted when the students from their class were there for two years. Everybody got roughly the same raise, and it was a great place to work, but you really couldn't differentiate yourself and that wasn't gonna work for me. I really wanted a place where I could, if I worked hard to differentiate to get ahead and achieve." Understanding Mark's mentality and motivation for wanting to get ahead and do the best he could for himself is a driving factor to how he was able to help create HBO Sports into the monster that it became. Not being able to make as much money because everyone was kind of on the same train tracks put him in a spot to go and look for other opportunities.

"So, I started to interview for jobs. Meanwhile, back at General Foods, every three months we do presentations. The finance guys do presentations to the assistant controllers and controllers of companies. I get a call one day from a gentleman named Andy Kaplan; he says, 'Mark, I don't know if you know me, I don't know if you remember me, I was the assistant comptroller at General Foods, I saw you do those presentations quarterly. I love the work you did. I now work at this new company called HBO.' I said, 'HBO, what is it?' He said, 'Oh, it's cable television and it's a movie channel; you buy movies and watch them on TV. We have some sports, we have some boxing, just get over here, this company is growing like crazy, we need young MBAs like you. Just get into the company in any track you can, it's gonna work out.'" Out of nowhere, the work Mark has been doing working on peas and carrots has now put him in a spot where he could work for a start-up television network where he'd be able to use the same skill sets he'd been fine-tuning and be able to differentiate himself. The HBO from thirty plus years ago was much different than the one we know and love today. While this choice seems like it would be pretty obvious now, it wasn't quite that easy back then.

"Going home, saying to my wife, 'I know that sounds like a big risk.' And we talked and I said, 'You know what, it'll give me a chance to get ahead.' The guy said, 'Come here and it'll work. The company is growing like a weed.'" Mark put his faith in himself and decided that the best thing he could do was try something out. If it didn't work out, he had built up enough equity in a giant corporation that he would be able to go back or go to a competitor and make the same money again. To make it to the top of one of these giant entities would have been much harder than getting into a start-up and bringing it to prominence.

Finding a company that not only allows you to do what is necessary for yourself and the company but will do whatever it takes to let the cream rise to the top is very important. "I took a job at HBO in the finance department where I actually had to do accounting and close the books every month for the sales and marketing. Lo and behold, the young man sitting in the cubicle next to me started about two weeks before me; his name was Rob Roth. Well, Rob was here. If you flash forward about twenty-five years. I'm running HBO pay-per-view and Rob is the CFO of HBO. I used to do his financial planning and analysis work, and he did my accounting work, and it was a great team, and twenty-five years later, we'll still love it." I don't believe that it was a coincidence that these two young men started at the same time and rose to become two of the most important people in the company. This just shows that finding the right spot can do wonders for you and for your company.

"I was in a company where you were in a box, and as great a company as it was, it didn't offer enough advancement quickly enough, it didn't offer a way to differentiate myself, and it didn't offer enough exposure outside of the job I was doing. Contrast that to HBO, a company that's growing like crazy. He came in, very little direction, and you had to run and run and run in any direction you could, and they allowed the best to find the right direction, put themselves in the right place, and make a successful career."

Mark was able to take advantage of a great situation. He was put into a spot where he could run in any direction and he realized there was a direction that spelled a lot of money for the company, which would mean a lot of money for him and more control over his career. "At the time, HBO had a young heavyweight fighter, Mike Tyson, and they were only about fifteen to eighteen fights into his career, and he hasn't even become heavyweight champion yet, and getting nearly three million dollars license fee per fight, which at that point was an incredible amount of money. And the deal was coming up, so I went out and studied the marketplace and interestingly at the time, most big fights, the biggest fights that today are the big pay-per-view blockbusters back then, they were on closed circuit television, you had to get in your car and drive to stadiums arenas, not sports bars and restaurants."

Reading that to yourself, it sounds ridiculous, right? Rather than being able to watch at your home or at a bar, you'd have to go to a stadium where the fight was even there. You'd watch on the jumbotron with the stadium speakers, which were much worse than they are today, and still need to pay for a ticket to get in. Thankfully, Mark was able to see that back then and change the game, literally. "I wrote the business plan and said we need to launch; pay-per-view company got approved internally.

I left my finance position and... I ran the pay-per-view business. And together, we launched in April 1991." They were able to get a huge fight on the card for this first go around, having two legends of boxing face off against each other: Evander Holyfield and George Foreman. Through right, promotion, marketing, and everything else, HBO spent thirty-four million dollars on the fight. For this first one, Mark was simply asked to generate more than they spent, so he had a target of thirty-five million dollars.

It wasn't quite as easy as saying you wanted something and letting the Internet or your phone do the rest. To receive premium cable channels like HBO was a process and a half. Each house that wanted to buy something on pay-per-view needed a specific box set up in their home. After some quick calculations, Mark realized that he grossly underestimated the number of boxes that were in circulation and he only had four months to figure out how they could get one million buys where there were only one hundred thousand homes that currently had these boxes in them.

"I went back to my office and I think I wet my pants and I said, 'Oh my god, we're going to lose a fortune. We're going to be out of business. I didn't think we could do one hundred thousand buys, and we needed a couple million to make our money back.' And I remember telling my bosses and they said, 'Well, young man, you better get to work, we have four months to make this happen.'" While this may have been very scary at the time, this allowed Mark to do whatever he could necessary to put together a plan of action and execute upon it to make sure that the project would succeed.

Knowing the financial side of things, Mark was able to put that part of his knowledge to use and negotiate with cable operators around the country. "I said, 'What do we have to do to get these boxes installed immediately and in huge number?' And the cable operator said, 'Well, you need to have a flow program that guarantees a cash flow.' So, I went back to New York and we put into place immediately a monthly pay-per-view fight series. Now at the time, the biggest fights from our fight was selling for thirty-five dollars. To make the premiere April 19, we decided to put a 19.95-dollar price tag on smaller monthly fights. We went out to the cable industry and they all said, 'Great, you'll guarantee us twelve fights a year.' We're in the time we launched that night on April 19, there were sixteen million boxes."

To think of how quickly so many people needed to move to get something like this completed is amazing. You need the cable operators to get their stuff together, HBO has to put everything into place, and then you need the customers to allow this to happen. But it did, and HBO saw great success from that night. "We did an eight percent by rate, sold 1.4 million pay-per-view buys for thirty-five million dollars, and generated fifty-three million dollars in one night." As you can imagine, helping the company in a positive way to the tune of about nineteen million dollars, Mark now had the chance to do what he wanted with his life and his place in the industry.

During Mark's time at the helm of HBO Sports Pay-Per-View, the product generated over 3.6 billion dollars in revenue and of sixty-five million PPV buys.[52] Mark has since left HBO and is currently helping specific boxers with their marketing and management needs to spread the sport he loves and to give the people in it a better chance.

---

52 Dan Rafael, "Mark Taffet to leave HBO at end of year," ESPN, November 24, 2015.

CHAPTER 10

Do as I Do

MAKE A LOT OF MONEY, HELP A LOT OF PEOPLE, HAVE A LOT OF FUN

David Meltzer is a shorter gentleman who always has a smile on his face. David has taught me a lot about being a good person, which I thought I was until I met him. There is so much we as people can do to help one another which we don't even think about from the surface level. David has helped with my business, he has helped me be accountable, he has helped me find the joy in all the things I do, and he helped me be a better interviewer (which is my favorite thing to do).

Dave is the co-founder of Sports 1 Marketing, a company he started with Hall of Fame quarterback Warren Moon. Sports 1 Marketing is a global marketing agency leveraging over twenty billion dollars in relationship capital. In Dave's words, "Sports 1 Marketing is a platform where we bring the right people, the right ideas to big sporting events and award shows and other things and it's allowed me to build big brands and work on big brands, both product brands and sporting brands from the NFLPA to huge companies and wheels up and, you know, Old Spice and just a variety of great companies all the way down to personal brands... like myself." This is the culmination of everything Dave has done up to this point, utilizing all the relationships, skills, knowledge, and experience he has acquired to put Sports 1 Marketing on the map. "I'm most proud of the platform's ability to build my brand and to attract what is the purpose of the company: which is to make a lot of money, which is to be abundant, to help a lot of people, which is to be abundant, and to have fun... Everyone should be focusing on what they can do to make a lot of money, what they can do to help a lot of people, and what they can do to have a lot of fun." Make a lot of money, help a lot of people, and have a lot of fun. Who says no to that kind of life?

He has started the Unstoppable Foundation, a non-profit humanitarian organization bringing sustainable education to children and communities in developing countries. He has a television show and podcast through *Entrepreneur Magazine*. He graduated from Tulane Law School and made one million dollars nine months after graduating. He was the CEO of Samsung's first smartphone division. He was the CEO of the most notable sports agency in the world, Leigh Steinberg Sports and Entertainment. He is a keynote speaker, author, business consultant, coach, and a personal friend of mine.

David preaches his four pillars in life: being grateful, accountability, empathy, and being connected to inspiration. If we all can live with these in mind each passing day, we will become better as a whole. David is also on a mission to impact a billion people to be happy, so if you are unfamiliar with him before this book, I hope I can help him impact you to be happy. Dave has also done a great job at getting me to understand what the most important things in life are in short order. One question he posed to me was "what would you do if time was not a factor?" Read that one more time for effect. The answer that came right to me was not what I was focusing most of my time on, and it got me to ask myself why I wasn't putting more time, energy, and effort into that? For me, it's interviewing people in sports to amplify their stories, experiences, and wisdom to help others learn. He then said if you put as much time into developing the skills, knowledge, and desire for that, you will become successful in the perfect amount of time. This is a huge reason why I wanted to write this book, and hopefully be able to spread these stories to anyone, including yourself, to help move you one step closer to your goal.

Dave grew up wanting to be an athlete, but as I said before, he's a bit shorter than many—if not all—of the professional athletes that we see today. So, the next best thing was to work in sports in some capacity. "My quantum being is not a great, talented athlete, but I had a joy of playing sports and I learned so much about it. It's the one thing that I call my cocoon. Sports, to me, was something that none of the people in my family did. Nobody expected me to even be decent at that, let alone good."

The lessons that we all can learn from playing sports at a young age like teamwork, hard work, and failure are all lessons we can carry throughout our lives. Learning them at a young age and bringing them with you wherever you go in life is a lot easier said than done, but if you do it right, you'll be thankful for it. "It was my cocoon because it strengthened every piece of my mental, spiritual, emotional, and physical being to pursue my potential within sports, and then I carried that over those lessons that I learned from playing sports all the way through college, and even getting a scholarship to play in college and overachieving as an average division three football player."Even though Dave was unable to become a world-class professional athlete, he is a world-class person with world-class advice. He was one of the first people I went to see to get a job in sports and he helped me do just that. "The first thing about getting a career in sports is to be more interested than interesting. I always tell people the story when I was eighteen that I wanted to be a doctor and didn't even know doctors had to work in hospitals. That's the way I feel that most people who want a career in sports; they look at sports at the surface. They watch a movie, and they say that's what I want to be, I want to be the GM of the Cubs, I want to be the manager of the Padres, I want to be a professional athlete, I want to be a sports agent."

Looking at many of these jobs and careers at the surface level is a dangerous thing to do. With sports being what we all love and use as a release, working in it quickly turns to "work," the exact opposite of the fun-loving activity you're used to. Plus, the movies really only show the fun parts, not the daily grind that it takes within that job, or all the hours put in on the way up the ladder to becoming the GM of the Cubs. "Remember sports is an industry. It's not a job. It's an industry like anything else.

And there's billions and billions of dollars in jobs within the sports industry."

Another thing I should mention about Dave is that he is a huge math guy. He believes that you can beat everyone and everything if you use math to your advantage instead of letting math take advantage of you.

"The way you can increase your statistical success to build a career in sports is to focus in on three things. The number one thing, your skills. Just like being an athlete, the best players get hired. They may not last if you don't work hard and do all these other things, but the people that are born with a quantum talent and are able to utilize that are the best players that have developed their skills. Secondly, knowledge. I still practice my skills... but knowledge is the second component. So many people have these dreams, and they have some skills, but they have no situational knowledge, experience advice, they have no mentorship, they're not willing to ask for help, and they're not willing to ask a series of questions to find out what they don't know.

"The biggest detriment I see with young people that want to grow in sports is they don't know what they don't know because they're not seeking knowledge, they're not seeking the most powerful thing in the world. There's no joke when people say knowledge is power. Knowledge is power for sure. We should always seek it. The best place to seek it is from people that sit in the situation that we want to be in, meaning they have the skills and the knowledge that we want, because they can accelerate that learning curve and also reduce the anxiety. They can help us practice in fear of the unknown, because we don't know too. The third component, and this is the one that's the magic sauce of sports, is desire. The thousand players that play in the MLB, the thirty-two managers and general managers and presidents, those are competitive. But the big differentiator is desire; the people who get those top jobs in any industry, they must be what they can be."

Developing the skills, knowledge, and desire of what you want in anything will help catapult your career and life forward. In terms of getting a job in sports, it will do the same. We know and understand that some talent is inherent, but that doesn't mean you still shouldn't practice every day. Knowledge of whatever you want, like being a GM and understanding how the front office works and why they made certain moves, will give you credibility when speaking about the subject. But most people forget about the desire part. That is what is going to drive someone to push harder and go further down that extra mile (the one that is usually emptiest) and do whatever it takes and more. The combination of these three attributes will help get you that job because not everyone is practicing these three things. Some people do two, others one, and some actually do all three but fall off before ninety-five percent of the way there and never make it.

Getting those top jobs are what we all covet, but you need to get your foot in the door first though, right? "The easiest way to enter sports, which is always the hardest part, where's my point of entry, is to provide value, meaning the bottom line." Essentially, if you can affect someone else's bottom line in a positive way, you will get a job within the sports industry. It may sound rudimentary, but it's a tale as old as time. As Dave said before, sports are an industry with billions of dollars in it. If you can help someone else make a percentage of that money, you will be able to enter the market in some capacity.

"For example, sports agency people... I'll tell you how to [become] a sports agent: affect the bottom line. How do you [affect] the bottom line, get a client and keep applying, but that's what being a sports agent [is] about. You can hire everybody else, everybody else will want to hire you if you keep getting clients and keeping clients." With all the opportunities that exist in the industry, as long as you can do one thing very well to affect the bottom line, you can surround yourself with others who do different things but also affect the bottom line in a positive way. "I have friends that do sponsorship, and when I went to them initially, I said, look, there's not a company or organization, a stadium, an arena, or an event that is going to turn me away if I come to them and say, 'Hey, I have a million dollars a sponsorship. Can I have twenty percent of it if I bring it to you?' Nobody's ever said no to me ever, but everybody likes to say I got this client, I got this. Like, I don't care." Letting ego get in the way of what matters most is another way to negatively affect yourself. Just because someone said you can help them doesn't mean anything if you aren't actually helping them! Affect the bottom line in the most positive way possible and you'll get that job you want.

"When you make money and prove that you are profit centers through skills, knowledge, and desire, and you bring and hit the bottom line, no doubt, you'll get the career in sports."

SKILLS, KNOWLEDGE, AND DESIRE

Figure out what you want to do! Then do everything you can to get better at it in all the ways possible. There might be different things along the way, too, but the easiest way to get a job in the sports industry, and to stay around long-term, is to develop skills, knowledge, and desire in an area that will affect the bottom line of a sports company. By effecting the bottom line, you will become a positive on the books instead of an expense.

This applies directly to me and what I'm trying to accomplish. Wanting to interview people as a career, I have been able to pinpoint the skills, knowledge, and desire that I need to get better at it. The only way you get paid in that line of work is if you're really, really good at it, so by taking time to get better at these things, I will eventually get to where I need to get paid.

PUSH FORWARD

Brandon Steiner is a legend in New York City sports. He is a fit older gentleman with a sweet jump shot (don't leave him open) and is always looking to help others, as you'll quickly find out. You'll normally find Brandon with a sports cap on, talking on the phone to someone he's looking to help. Brandon is also a speaker, author, and coach.

Brandon is best known for his work with the New York Yankees, as well as other New York sports figures. He started his first business, Steiner Sports, in 1987 to help sports stars partner with brands and businesses to help drive traffic to their stores and companies. He knew that sports fans would do anything to meet and know their favorite athletes, so by bringing them places that were looking to drive traffic and associate with these athletes, he was able to create win-win-win situations. Outside of just appearances, Brandon got good at marketing athletes and created higher-level partnership deals that would allow for even bigger wins for all sides.

Getting started, for many different businesses, start with small wins all over the place to continue to drive your passion forward and get you to see that there is success in the idea. "Everybody needs help. Regardless how famous and rich you are, everybody needs help. Now some people don't like to admit it and there have been a lot of stubborn athletes over the years, but everyone needs help. When I got an opportunity to work with Derek Jeter in the '90s, he was putting his foundation together and that's where my focus was, not on if I could make money." Looking for a way to help a young guy with his foundation so he could help others, being the major focus will lead to where it needs to go. When starting a business, especially in sports, you first need clients before you can do anything! By understanding how he could gain a client, help a lot of people, and do good, he was able to work with one of the greatest baseball players of all time.

"I thought it would be really good to be able to do some marketing with them, but in the mid-'90s I was a young kid, but I figured let me take a chance. Mariano was having a hard time speaking English and kind of getting around, helping with a lot of little things with travel car services. I didn't know he was gonna end up being

Mariano Rivera. I look like a genius now, you know, having worked with him for the last twenty-five years, but I'm like 'I didn't know.' But you know you get a good feeling about a person and that's very important, you know, I try to work with people I like that are good people."

Helping a guy out when he needs it in whatever way he could led Brandon Steiner to work with arguably the best relief pitcher of all time. This helped him develop a relationship with him and now he's been able to work with him for over twenty-five years by just being a good person.

To no surprise, helping people leads to other people hearing and seeing that. "I remember working with Yogi Berra, and I killed myself for Yogi. I did so many things back in the early '90s, getting started working with him, it was like a blessing and he's amazing. And one day I got a call from his sons and they said, 'We're taking over all his marketing and if you want anything, call us.' I was devastated, really bummed, but I had done everything this guy possibly could." Sometimes everything doesn't quite work out the way you think it will. But understanding the long game, understanding that you need to do whatever it takes and sometimes it's not enough, and understanding there is more helps you get over the bad things that can come. Getting fired by a legend like Yogi Berra has to be one of the worst feelings in the world.

"I couldn't believe that I was now going to be someone on the outside, but then, two years later, Phil Rizzuto out of nowhere, I get his call for the whole business from the Veterans Committee, and everybody's trying to get Phil to sign up with them for marketing and there hasn't been a Hall of Famer on the Yankees in a while then, it was '94. The Yankees weren't that good at that point, so getting Phil Rizzuto was a big deal. And I was competing against a lot of big companies and people that have been there a while, and I was sitting in the living room, trying to pitch him and Cora, his wife, and I'm like, man, I gotta get this. I'm gonna get this. And then, like two days later, Phil calls and says, 'Steiner, I'm gonna go with you.' And some time later he had said, 'Listen, the reason why I went with you is because I was talking to Yogi and, you probably don't know that Yogi and I are very good friends, Yogi said all the stuff that you've done for him and if I was going to do a marketing thing with somebody that I should do a deal with you because nobody's gonna work harder for me than you.'" Doing good work always leads to more work. You might not know where it comes from, or how you get it, or why you even get it, but make sure you're always doing the best you can for your clients and those around you.

"So, even though it didn't end exactly where I wanted to with Yogi, it's funny, years later I end up getting back with Yogi and his kids and end up doing all this stuff for the last five, six years when he was alive so that was a blessing too. You just kind of focus on doing good quality work and get better every day and try to do more and as much as you can for as many people. And I think it's, like, I didn't really know what I was into. I was just trying to hook Yogi up so I could pay my rent, you know what I mean? Like I was always trying to hustle and come up with really good ideas and here he is giving a testimonial to help me, which I didn't even know. And then Phil ends up signing with me as opposed to like thirty other people that are trying to sign him and that was a big break in my career, man, so you don't know where the breaking transition is going to come in. But you do know that you put as much good out there as you can."

Brandon has since left his original business, Steiner Sports, and has blazed another trail with his new agency and collectible business. Brandon has recreated himself and now has CollectibleXchange, where he is able to help people buy and sell sports memorabilia as well as other collectibles online, as well as starting up The Steiner Agency, where he does much of the same things he was at Steiner Sports!

LEARN BY EXAMPLE

The saying usually goes "lead by example," and these gentlemen clearly believe that. Now it's up to you to learn by their example. Their ideas may not be revolutionary, but they're a reminder that if there is something you want to do, you need to develop the skills, knowledge, and desire around that pursuit. This will give you the best understanding of how to execute at the highest level for that. You can also take the idea of hard work, no matter what, for whoever you can, to learn that business can come from many different places and be many different things. Yes, the chances you start helping out two Hall of Famers before their careers really get going is slim, but doing it because you want to help will eventually lead to more business. People talk and the sports industry isn't as big as we're meant to believe!

PART 3

CHAPTER 11

High School, College, and Career Changers

―――――

I hope you had an enjoyable time with this book. It was a blast for me to interview the amazing guests, hear their stories, and put them down on paper for you to learn from! There are a few different stories in this book that can apply to everyone, there are stories from people who grew up in the sports world, and other who didn't get in until they were well into their careers. One lesson everyone will be able to learn from this book is that you should not be expecting to get paid for something you've never done before! So, start doing it for free on your own; the Internet exists so I don't believe you when you say you can't. Plus, just about any career you can think of already exists in the sports world. Lawyers, accountants, healthcare workers, and etcetera all have places within teams, leagues, and companies that cater to the sports industry.

I want you to understand that this book is for people of all ages! If you're in high school, hopefully you can understand the industry more and what's needed of you before you pick a college to go to. If you're in college, I hope that this can give you a better understanding of what you'll need to do before you even make your first dollar. And for our career changers, congrats to you! I've changed careers already and I'm much happier that I did! Getting into sports sounds like a fun thing, and it is, especially if you hated what you were doing before. So, I hope you career changers enjoy this book too! Understand where other people came from and how they were able to apply their skills, knowledge, and desires to an industry they're actually interested in.

High Schoolers: Don't fret too much! There is a lot of life to live, also on a side note, high school *is* important, but I promise you it's not nearly as important as you think it is. You'll learn that after you go to college. That being said, start to dabble. You may have an idea of what you'd like to do, but it's probably better that you learn a few different things now that you like and apply them to sports. You like math? Awesome, analytics are huge in just about all sports organizations. You enjoy writing? Well, fire up that blog! Think being an anchor would be fun or want to be on the radio? Livestream some videos or start a podcast. The world is your oyster. Yes, you'll probably be embarrassed and people might snicker behind your back, but those same people will be asking you how you did after you've put in five years of work and have a way cooler job than them right out of college! When looking for a school, make sure you're going to a school that just has sports. Giant D1 school vs. small D3 doesn't matter. The competition might be harder at those bigger schools for you to find your way in.

College Kids: Enjoy the heck out of these four years, they are the best of your life (at least mine), but it only gets worse if you want it to. Make sure to get involved with something in sports business. You don't have to be a student manager for the football team, but I can guarantee that there is some spot of sports business club. If there isn't, that's even better because it means you can create one! The reason you want to do this is because the sports business industry is very competitive. As we've been saying, high supply and high demand. So, your resume might be awesome, but if it's in a stack of papers, it's going to get lost. Become a part of one of these groups and meet as many people as you can! Be nice, have real conversations, and create relationships. Everyone knows somebody. By building your network and befriending more and more people, you'll have a better shot at connecting with someone who can get you in touch with the hiring manager at your favorite company. Also, internships are very important, as I'm sure you've already been told. So again, network a lot at those places as well so you can start making friends with the people who are around you and the people who are higher up. Start with people on your level because they will all go to other companies where they will have open positions one day. Then make sure to meet the people who are a level or two up because they know more people!

Career Changers: The first step is going to be the hardest, of course. Unless you're coming from an even more specific industry (think aerospace engineer), there won't be as many open positions as you'd like. They also are probably in places you have never thought to live in. Whatever you're doing, start looking to those things in the sports industry. You're an accountant and want to work in sports? Athletes, teams, and leagues all need accountants! Looking to change what you do completely? Well, that might be a bit harder, but a side hustle never hurt anyone! I can't comment on where you are in your life, but I can say you will probably be happier doing something in the sports world, which means more to me than anything else.

Overall, I think this book can help a significant number of people and bring light to how being a good person can actually help you get ahead in the world of sports. You get your dream job with some great people helping, a lot of hard work, and being a bit smarter than everyone else. I get the satisfaction of helping others and hopefully inspiring the next great sports talent!

If you have any questions, don't hesitate to reach out to me through email michael.rasile1@gmail.com and shoot me any messages you have on Twitter @michaelrasile1.

Acknowledgments

I never thought I would be the kind of person who wanted to write a book, and when I did have a small glimmer in my eye to write one, I didn't think it would be quite like this. Thankfully, I've always loved talking to people and asking questions. This led me to interviewing others with a microphone, and eventually to me transcribing some of the best conversations I had!

I want to thank my family and friends for their support through the project! When I told everyone about it, I was amazed by how excited and happy everyone was for me, which helped make this book even more incredible! My parents Michael and Kim, my brother CJ, my wife Katelyn, my cousin Justin, and my friends that I consider family, Nick, Jeremy, Brenna, Megan, Derek, Xtina, among others!

I want to thank all of the amazing guests that have given me their time and allowed me to do my favorite thing in the world, asking questions! I appreciate each and every one that allowed me to have them in the book and bring some of their stories, experience, and wisdom to some more people in the world!

Shout-out to the New Degree Press Team, my editors Kim and Al, as well as Brian and Eric who all had their hands all over this thing!

Here is a list of the incredible people who contributed to my efforts in writing a book!

Katelyn Ribbecke

Kathy and Brian Ribbecke

Kim and Michael Rasile

Michelle Cselovszky and Brian Ribbecke

Jason Yuhas

Mitch Howard

Nick Bretwisch

CJ Rasile

Sia Nejad

Joseph E. Storzinger

Alycia Powell

Danielle Puleo

Fabio Faschi

Pat Smith

Terron Tidwell

Jim Swanton

Joseph Dupriest

Brenna Sprella and Nick Wright

Christina Crawford and Derek Rampulla

Timothy Peterson

Jason Mezrahi

Brad Chabra

Tim Scanlan

Zachary Smith

Dr. Brett Guimard

Andrew Leone

Andrew Diamond

Sarah Schaible

Scott San Emeterio

Marissa Marzano and Adam Freitag

Alen Silverrstieen

Sarah Schaible

Sebastian Marentes

Sam, Sumner, and Baby Sumner Siecke

Justin Rasile

James Fiorentino

Lauren Houghton

Derek Longenecker

Sam Schaible

Joseph Brenner

Dexter Conner

Jake Miller

Anthony Laudato

Adam Posner

Michael Willett

David Jaffin

Eric Koester

Rosemary Rosencrans

Ryan Delaney

Amanda McGrew

Paul O'Connor

Alex Pitocchelli

Nicholas Di Tommaso

Cody Darwick

John Balkam

Aaron Siegal-Eisman

Rob Cressy

James Sheridan

Benjamin Fairclough

Doug Klein

Nicholas D'Souza

Brennen Forster

Alex Onaindia

Salman Hasan

Alexander Amir

Drew Danzeisen

Megan Latimer

Colleen Maloy

Tera Bradham DeNeui

Randall Thompson

David Kagulu-Kalema

Eric Spyropoulos

Nick Hayden

Jake Fleshner

Matthew Barry

Appendix

INTRODUCTION:

i9 Sports. "How Large Is the Industry?" Accessed September 9, 2020.

Plunkett Research. "Sports Industry Statistic and Market Size Overview, Business and Industry Statistics." Accessed September 9, 2020.

SportyCo. "How Big is the Sports Industry?" Accessed September 9, 2020.

CHAPTER 1

Medical Press. "Men's Testosterone Levels Predict Competitiveness," University of Texas at Austin. Accessed: September 9, 2020.

NCAA. "Estimated probability of competing in college athletics." Accessed September 9, 2020.

Psychology Research and Reference. "Competition in Sports." Accessed September 9, 2020.

Rovell, Daren. "How 'Jerry Maguire' Ruined the Sports Agency Industry." ESPN, Dec 13, 2016.

CHAPTER 2

Grant, Adam M. *Give and Take: A Revolutionary Approach to Success*. New York, N.Y.: Viking. 2013.

CHAPTER 3

Zippia. "ESPN Careers & Jobs." Accessed September 9, 2020.

CHAPTER 4

Farmer, Sam. "Profootballtalk.com Acquired by NBC." LA Times, June 15, 2009.

Fuentes, Jon. "Joe Rogan Reveals How He Became The Voice Of UFC." MMA News. February 6, 2019.

Luino, Marc. "Giraffe Neck Marc." Accessed Mar 25, 2015, YouTube Channel.

Reinsmith, Trent. "With Dana White's Claim That The UFC Is Worth $7 Billion, It's Time To Revisit Fighter Pay." Forbes. Aug 21, 2018.

Rock, David 'DRock'. "How I Got My Job For Gary Vaynerchuk." *Medium*. Jun 1, 2017.

CHAPTER 5

Eisenband, Jeff. "Bartending, Country Music and Kay Adams' Relentless Path to Success." *Front Office Sports*. February 1, 2019.

Hildalgo, Carlos. "I Used to Believe in Hustle Porn, and Now I Think it's the Antithesis of the American Dream." *Fast Company*. June 20, 2019.

Paramo, Daniel. "Gender Inequality in Sports Broadcasting Apparent to Viewers." *The Daily Evergreen*. October 5, 2017.

Podgorny, D.J. "Ian Rapoport: Relentlessly Competitive." *Front Office Sports*, November 7, 2016.

CHAPTER 7

Podgorny, D.J. "Ian Rapoport: Relentlessly Competitive." *Front Office Sports*, November 7, 2016.

CHAPTER 8

Hodges, Cassie Ann. "US Venture Capital Investment Surpasses $130 Billion in 2019 for Second Consecutive Year." NVCA. January 14, 2020.

SeventySix Capital. "SeventySix Capital names Jessica Romanelli Director of Digital Marketing." April 27, 2017.

CHAPTER 9

Legal Sports Report. "US Sports Betting Revenue and Handle." Last Updated: October 12, 2020.

Rafael, Dan. "Mark Taffet to leave HBO at end of year." *ESPN*, November 24, 2015.

CPSIA information can be obtained
at www.ICGtesting.com
Printed in the USA
BVHW090417211220
596045BV00006B/17